DAVID ADJAYE
CONSTRUCTED
NARRATIVES

David Adjaye

DAVID ADJAYE CONSTRUCTED NARRATIVES

Edited by Peter Allison

Lars Müller Publishers

To my mother, Cecilia Twum Adjaye,
for her love and patience

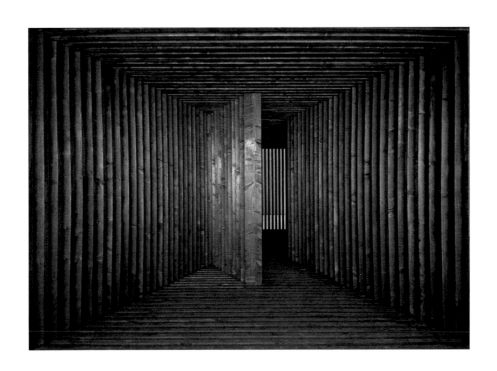

Horizon, London, 2007

This book is a reflection on the architectural investigations that we have been involved in for the past twenty years, an attempt to understand the work through a series of reflections. The completion of the National Museum of African American History and Culture in Washington, DC, is a wonderful moment to look back on the work, but I am equally interested in our early prototypes and tests. To understand the impact of these constructions needed time, and now it is possible to see the roles they have played in projects that are in daily use – rather than their significance as theoretical propositions. It is like the difference between photographs taken at the time that a building is first completed and those taken after it has had time to bed in. The later images always have more atmosphere, as people have found their own ways of occupying the spaces. It is at this point that one can begin to take stock. The design of the museum is the culmination of a long process; if you look at the way in which our work has built up, it is the outcome of a natural progression. What is unique about the museum is the incredible site and the charged narrative behind the premise on which it is built, and these conditions allowed our previous investigations to have a bigger resonance.

We started the book two years ago, when Peter Allison and I met Lars Müller in Zurich to discuss the themes that had been going through my mind. The chapters that we decided on at the meeting look at the kinds of questions that I grapple with when I am working. My intention was to amplify these areas, which you can see in the projects themselves, to allow others to have a view on some of my preoccupations. All of the books I have made have developed out of a particular set of circumstances. The *David Adjaye: Houses* book was a kind of manual. We had been working intensely on private commissions in London, and by collecting the projects together, I wanted to assess the different design strategies we had deployed. The second book, *David Adjaye: Making Public Buildings,* was the first test of a thesis. It was connected with having an opportunity to exhibit a number of public buildings before most of them were completed, so the book was a work of speculation, a document about the intentions behind the projects. The third book, *Adjaye Africa Architecture,* developed from a series of visits to African cities, and was about creating an archive. This was the reason I was keen for the 2011 edition to be published as a seven-volume boxed set; it is like a small library – an index that begins to cross reference a range of phenomena. It was the first archival book I made and was conceived as a stand-alone element that could give birth to many subsets.

Lars Müller has become the quintessential publisher of ideas books. In a field that has become very reduced, he is someone with a strong graphic ideology who publishes books that reveal the enquiry behind why things are made. When we discussed this book, it was generous of him not to question our intentions and instead proceed to interrogate how things should be put together – the relationships, and the compositional tensions. In the book itself, the way that images have been cropped and the relative casualness or formality with which images have been used derive from Lars. The book deals with strong design statements but treats them with a certain informality and ease, which is due to his influence. In his studio, Esther Butterworth developed a graphic strategy covering all aspects of the book, and Muriel Blancho guided the text through copy editing and onto the page. Their input was invaluable and we appreciated their collaborative approach. In our London office, I would like to thank Michael Matey and Iris Sastre-Rivero for their assistance with images of the work. Finally, my thanks are due to Peter Allison for his editorial input on the text and visual material.

The combination of text and images is meant to provide a window on the work because, if I am honest, I am not that interested in trying to fully explain exactly what I am doing in words. I resist doing that because it is a slippery slope, but I am interested in giving leads to a possible explanation. It is important to me that the essays in the book are open-ended – they are ways to under-stand the routes that I have taken and where they might lead.

David Adjaye

GEO-graphics: A map of art practices in Africa, past and present, exhibition at Bozar, Brussels, 2010 (artistic director, David Adjaye)

GEOGRAPHY AND ARCHITECTURE IN AFRICA

_GEOGRAPHIC TERRAINS

The notion that architecture has the capacity to make sensitive contributions in a range of situations around the world is one I have been increasingly drawn to. I have always been fascinated by the global mutations of modern architecture on different continents, and I am constantly being drawn back to this type of hybrid architecture. Whether in Japan, South America, or India, modern architecture evolved in surprising ways as it encountered different cultural and climatic conditions from those in which it first developed. The creative moment, when a general model is brought face-to-face with a set of highly specific conditions, is an opportunity for innovation, for questioning established scenarios and developing new models. When you have this oscillation between a universal idea and a condition on the ground, the resulting work never becomes decoupled and self-contained. In the process of adapting to the location, it remains part of a wider discourse.

_The connection between geography and architecture was one of the things I looked at in my study of the architecture and urbanism of Africa's capital cities. I decided to embark on the study because I felt that Africa was often seen as an exotic place that had become disconnected from the rest of the world, a troubled continent that had little to offer. Having been brought up there, I saw it rather differently – as a place where every possible variant had been produced and every relationship had been contested. Colonialism, for example, is often assumed to have had similar consequences in different cities, which was not the case at the time or now, as the cities continue to develop. By immersing myself in the experience of the cities, I began to notice tendencies and patterns. Some of the places I visited seemed quite bizarre, but as I looked more closely, I could see how they responded to the conditions in different climatic zones. This was the basis for classifying all the cities according to their position in one of six "geographic terrains," a term that is intended to suggest the interaction between a set of general conditions and a specific location.

_In each city, I photographed representative building types and made a record of what I saw in the streets and open spaces. The overview in the book is based on combining these images in a loose order, which can be understood in two different ways.[1] As I collected the material in a relatively short period, it provides a record of the cities at a particular time and can therefore be used as a reference point for studying their future development. Showing buildings of different generations coming up to the present, and examples of recent informal developments, it also illustrates patterns of development that are likely to extend into the future. As the rate of urbanization in Africa continues to rise, tracking these patterns will be an essential tool in developing strategies for the future of these cities.

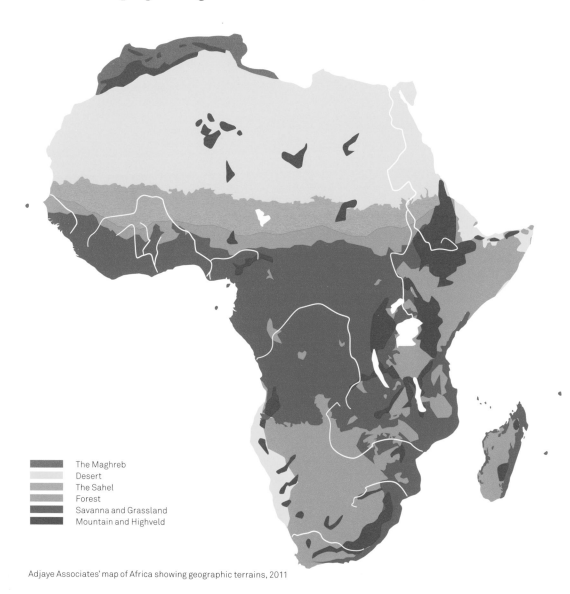

The Maghreb
Desert
The Sahel
Forest
Savanna and Grassland
Mountain and Highveld

Adjaye Associates' map of Africa showing geographic terrains, 2011

_The introductions to each of the geographic terrains provide basic climatic data: temperature range, seasonal rainfall, and their effects on the vegetation and landscape. But in the cities I was more concerned with recording the human response to these conditions, as reflected in civic, commercial, and residential buildings, and the way in which external spaces were used. Rather than making a physical analysis, I wanted to understand the impact of climate on the lifestyle of the people, their attitude to place, and how they occupied space in response to the prevalent conditions. My conclusion is that the way of life in these places is a precise response to climate, and shows how buildings can adapt to climate without becoming overly dependent on technology. With the increasing use of air conditioning, it is worth remembering that many people still live and work in buildings that are constructed in very basic materials.

_Much of the vernacular building in Africa is a direct response to climate: the tightly clustered houses of the medinas in the cities of the Maghreb, which keep the narrow lanes and the lower floors in shade; the mud-brick houses of the Sahel, with thick walls and small openings to protect the interior from the strength of the sun, or the deep verandas of houses in the Forest region, which protect the external walls from torrential rain, allowing doors and windows to remain open for ventilation. More recently, colonial and postcolonial architecture in the Forest and the Savanna and Grassland regions has seen a proliferation of buildings with pierced screens and solar shading devices, which dominate the exterior at the expense of conventional doors and windows. In my photographs I was interested in recording how such devices reduce glare and soften the effects of the harsh light. The atmosphere they create is the first thing one experiences. In developing projects in different geographic locations, I have had reason to remember these striking examples of climate moderation.

_HYBRIDIZATION

The cultural phenomenon that reflects my initial perception of the continent as a place of many intersecting histories is that

Tuti Island (left), confluence of the White and Blue Nile Rivers, Khartoum, Sudan, Desert

View toward the Nation Centre Building, Nairobi, Kenya, Mountain and Highveld

Kenneth Scott, Scott House, Accra, Ghana, Forest, 1961   ⟩

Protected facades, Pretoria, South Africa, Savanna and Grassland

Brick-clad tower, Bamako, Mali, The Sahel

Thatched house, Bissau, Guinea Bissau, Forest

of hybridization. A period in which the main ethnic groups occupied specific areas was followed, in the last millennium, by one in which they migrated and interacted with other groups. This process was accelerated by more recent contact with the outside world through slavery, colonialism, international developments in the postcolonial era, and population movement from rural areas to the cities. These sweeping changes are reflected in the increasing hybridization of the urban environment: cities with distinctive quarters whose organization stems from the culture of their original inhabitants; areas that have been abandoned by one population and reoccupied by another; eclectic combinations of buildings with different cultural sources, and buildings that mix indigenous and international motifs. Two of my favorite examples are the people of Asmara enjoying the *passeggiata* in the arcaded streets built by Italian colonizers, and the multi-faith skyline of Kampala, with the grand mosque, a Sikh temple, and two cathedrals, each one standing on a separate hilltop.

_I am interested in hybridization as an indicator of cultural change and include hybrid elements in my work to make it accessible to a wider audience. The design of the National Museum of African American History and Culture involves the introduction of a hybrid form – a crown-like superstructure based on a Yoruba sculpture from Nigeria – in the context of the National Mall. Although it might appear to be an intrusion, it is intended to complement the existing buildings. The angled profile of my building is represented in the nearby Washington Monument, but before our building was constructed, the monument was the exception to everything around it. By contextualizing the monument, we hope to show how the cultural system represented by the other buildings on the Mall is not as autonomous as it first appears, and how that tradition connects with other systems.

_From the outside, Africa may look like a *tabula rasa*, the site of a long line of experiments that have little to do with each other, but closer acquaintance confirms that it is contested ground where the local conditions have been transformed by outside forces. This has echoes in the wider world, where the effects of globalization have undermined the identity of familiar places. In most of the situations I look at as an architect, many histories overlap, and I try to avoid the temptation to draw out one of them at the expense of the others. Rather than responding to physical traces, I prefer to extrapolate the emotive conditions suggested by earlier narratives. These may involve setting up a sense of denial, of opportunity, reflection, aloofness, or conviviality, any of which can contribute to the atmosphere of the building – the device that first communicates what a building has to offer.

_My desire to understand the attributes of African cities by classifying them in groups does not entirely recognize the nature of some of their differences. Earlier in their history many of the capitals had strong international links, which have remained equally or more significant since independence. In the case of Accra in the 1950s and 1960s, for example, President Nkrumah began to restructure the city in response to its new status as the capital of a republic that would play a significant role within Africa and on the world stage. This double orientation, inward to the country and outward to the rest of the globe, can be seen in many capitals but is a feature of the African cities, which are often separated by great distances. The specific orientation of the African cities, and the strength of their external connections, can make a significant difference to the identities of cities in the same geographic terrain.

_In the contemporary world, cities are widely understood in terms of their physical infrastructure, development patterns, and the character of their buildings. Upper Harlem, the National Mall in Washington, DC, and Beirut's waterfront are all places that are known and appreciated on this basis. In wishing to address the expectations of a diverse public, I am interested in moving away from a position where architecture is judged in terms of a single criterion of progress, to one in which several scenarios can be considered at the same time.

1 David Adjaye, *Adjaye Africa Architecture: A Photographic Survey of Metropolitan Architecture*, ed. Peter Allison (Thames and Hudson, 2011 and 2016), also published as *African Metropolitan Architecture* (Rizzoli, 2011).
An earlier version of this essay was published in *Architecture is Life*, ed. Mohsen Mostafavi (Lars Müller Publishers, 2013).

GEOGRAPHY AND
ARCHITECTURE IN AFRICA

AFRICAN
CITIES

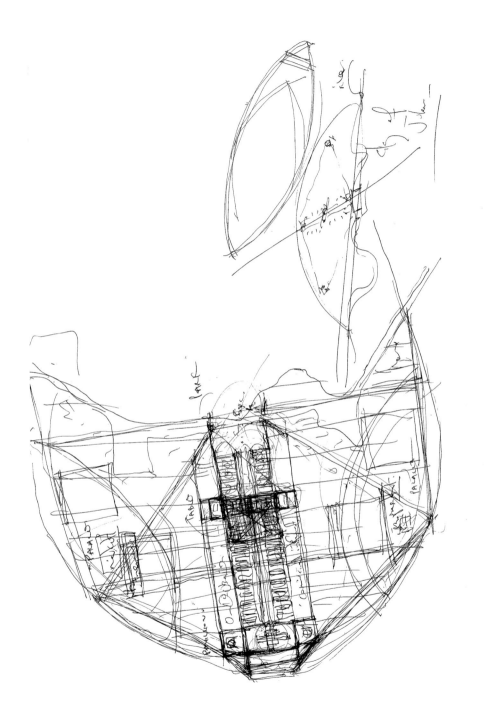

Study for master plan, Juba, South Sudan, 2012

The medina, Algiers, Algeria   Souk, Tunis, Tunisia

The French city, Rabat, Morocco

Bourlier, Ferrer-Laloé, and Miquel, Aéro-Habitat building, Algiers, Algeria, 1955

Tripoli, Libya

Cairo, Egypt

University of Khartoum, Khartoum, Sudan

Bank building, Djibouti, Djibouti

Mosque, Nouakchott, Mauritania

Bamako, Mali

Residential street, Ouagadougou, Burkina Faso

Geometric facade, Niamey, Niger

Place des Cinéastes, Ouagadougou, Burkina Faso

Kampala, Uganda

Market, Lilongwe, Malawi

Projecting balcony, Bissau, Guinea Bissau

Pancho Guedes, Abreu Santos e Rocha Building, Maputo, 1953

Black Star Monument, Accra, Ghana, 1961

Abuja, Nigeria

Pedestrian avenue, Gaborone, Botswana

El Mansour Building, Dakar, Senegal

Geometric facade, Dakar, Senegal

Addis Ababa, Ethiopia

Italian colonnades, Asmara, Eritrea

Amyas Connell, Sharia House, Nairobi, Kenya, 1979

Corrugated roofs, Kibera, Nairobi, Kenya

TALKING ABOUT FORM

_HORIZON

The Horizon pavilion was conceived at a time when I was thinking about exhibition design and wanted to show something about my architecture without making a representation of an actual project. My intention was to set up a one-to-one experience for visitors, to draw them into a structure that would show how construction can frame ideas. I hoped that, by removing most of the practical issues you find in a normal design brief, Horizon would succeed in making the connection between construction and ideas more visible than it might be in a conventional building. A conceptual idea can inform construction in a very precise way, independently of any practical requirements. What I am really talking about is form: the concept leads to a form, the concept defines a form, and the construction frames that form. Form is not just derived from program or function; it can also be derived from context. An understanding about context can be a concept, independent from construction but informed by it. There are many ways of constructing something, but once the conceptual idea is figured out, it is possible to develop a relationship between the construction and the form.

_Horizon represents the type of meta-thinking that should be located in an open field, framing a view. A field would have been an ideal setting, but I had been invited to work in a room in a basement, a completely enclosed space, so I needed to organize a view internally. I definitely did not want people to think that the Horizon was a self-referential exercise about construction, so it was important to show that the system represented by the construction was predicated on something else, which was the view. This was why I needed the image of the Sea of Galilee to complete the scenario. You start with the idea of gazing across a landscape, and the form is a construction that frames the gaze. This is the theme in all my pavilions – they speak to a way of making form and construction specific to a requirement, where architecture only has to mediate between a person and some other phenomenon. In Horizon the architecture mediates a special kind of view, an idyllic view. There are other possibilities, but in this case I defined "idyllic" as an empty view of

nature, an atmosphere that I thought was conceptually powerful – I was collapsing architecture into nature, into that atmosphere. In this type of project, I am talking about architecture
and being, about inhabiting the view, which for me is the perfect situation.

_In parallel with developing the structure of Horizon, my broth-
er Peter Adjaye composed a soundtrack, to be played through
speakers mounted on the roof. My collaboration with Peter
is interesting because I can observe how another constructed
form – not physical but sound form – can be visualized and
understood acoustically, alongside the architecture. I am
intrigued by this relationship between the acoustic and the
visual. Peter creates melodic structures in sound and his music
for Horizon provided an alternative view of the concept that
is the heart of this project, which hinges on the way that com-
pression and expansion can set up a specific relationship to an
overview. This was our theme, experiencing the three-dimensional notion of the portal.

_The slotted structure of Horizon is a development of the form
of construction I had employed in two earlier pavilions, Asymmetric Chamber and Length × Width × Height. It is part of
a long study I have been engaged in, exploring systems of
construction based on a single detail. In Horizon the system
reduces construction to two axes, the x- and y-axes, and a very
singular act involving the most basic joining of two planes. The
larger study is about looking for purity in construction, and
this pavilion is an attempt to put one example into practice.
What happens when you commit to that primary act? How
much variation can you make on this basis? In Horizon it is
about horizontal variety, where the creative act concerns splitting. If the final frame, just before the view, marks a split
between two worlds, how much splitting would take you back
to the moment of engagement? It is a structure based on using
repetition as a basis for modulating a single concept, a structure whose elements represent time.

_Horizon was the first occasion that I used a dark stain to
mute the color and grain of the timber. The earlier pavilions
were emphatic timber constructions, and as much as that was

beautiful and powerful, I was drawn to a different analysis. The physical reality of the material is important, but I wanted the emphasis to be on the presence of construction, the presence of material when it is used in a particular way. As I moved forward, untreated planed timber started to feel like a device that was fighting the end game that I had in mind, because it set up a pleasurable interior in its own right. I was not trying to create an interior but a portal to a view. Darkening the timber puts the emphasis on the splitting action, casting a shadow on the presence of the timber. It is not overpowering but has a gentle, reassuring presence.

_All of the pavilion structures are part of an ongoing exercise, in which we learn from one as we do the next. There is a direct relationship between Asymmetric Chamber and Horizon, in the sense that they both respond to similar ideas and share my thinking about the splitting of time and the splitting of construction. The splitting of construction is first explored in Asymmetric Chamber, a pavilion that extended the experience of a ten-meter-long space over a distance of thirty meters, which was the maximum I could fit into the gallery. In Length × Width × Height the notion of this measuring device is then tested in a specific urban context. The site was over thirty meters long, and I could make a single bar that would register the ground- and the sky-plane – in relation to the human body, this struck me as empirically and spatially interesting. The main difference between the earlier projects and Horizon is that they were organized on a strictly linear basis, while the angled geometry of Horizon, and later pavilions, responds to a view.

_FRAMING DEVICES

My interest in framing devices that create a sense of perspective goes back to my studies in Kyoto in the early 1990s. Many of the entrance sequences to temple complexes function in this way, with gateways that separate you from the outside world and lead you to the temple house. Sometimes they take the form of markers along the route, and in other examples they cluster together to focus the eye. I am fascinated by the hit-and-miss pattern of the timber construction of Horizon. It suggests a primary act, a direct approach to the act of building, but it results in a highly legible abstraction that is completely removed from the reality of construction. The possibility of making an equivalence between the essential act of building and what that construction can represent, as an abstract system, is very important to me. It functions as an open invitation to enter an intermediate zone between two different worlds. Escaping the restrictions that apply at either pole allows me to explore the identity of a project, without it being determined in advance by the materials or systems I am working with.

_At the time I designed Horizon we were working on the Stephen Lawrence Centre, which also incorporates triangular forms, and I am sure that there are many connections between these conceptual tests. I remember the moment when I realized that the two triangles at Stephen Lawrence could resolve the various issues presented by the site, and that architecturally they made a kind of embrace. Adding a device that represents time, in the pavilion, gave me a better understanding of the triangle as a form. I was not referencing one project in the other, but the triangle has definitely become part of my formal language. I am exploring almost all the Euclidean forms and understanding them through the lens of different construction techniques, understanding them beyond just pure form and light, as a basis for perceiving the world. I am committed to exploring these Euclidean geometries and what they are capable of in different contexts. If you look at the body of my work, I am fascinated by the square, the circle, and the triangle. They figure in all the projects, but the pavilions provide an opportunity to study their essential properties.

_As it is demountable in sections, Horizon has been shown in several venues, and it was interesting to see how it operates in different situations. In the Albion Gallery in London, where Horizon was first shown in 2007, it had a very direct relationship to the room in which it stood. There was a dichotomy here because my structure was so completely enclosed. I thought I had designed a framing device, but because it occupied a large part of the available space, it felt like one hermetic box inside another. In Munich the gallery was more open, and there was more space for the notion of the gaze to come into play. At Albion, and when it was shown at the British School in Rome in 2008, the image of Lake Galilee was incorporated in a laminated glass wall that was an integral part of the pavilion. When we showed Horizon at Munich's Haus der Kunst in 2015, we separated the image from the structure of the pavilion, which opened up the relationships between the pavilion and the gallery in a way that I really enjoyed. In this arrangement the architecture of the pavilion became more invisible, whereas at Albion the construction was the dominant feature, as if I was forcing the narrative. The perception may have been purer and more precise in London, but I preferred the situation in Munich. I love the idea that architecture is an armature to something else, so that you are unaware of being pushed in a particular direction – you might know something is happening, but you do not have to decide whether you go with it or not. The decoupling of the image from the structure in Munich allowed for that seduction to take place. I was surprised but, on balance, everything was clearer there. I would like to see it framing a view in a real landscape, like Specere, the pavilion that we built in the Kielder Forest, or Ephemeropterae, the pavilion in a Baroque park in Vienna.

_THE MONOFORMS

In the places we have shown it, Horizon has always been accompanied by the Monoforms furniture series, which I completed at the same time. Conceptually, they are two parts of the same proposition, but they are articulated in very different ways. Both involve a deliberate reduction in the complexity of the program, but in the Monoforms I retained the idea that furniture was part of the exercise. Although they have a human scale, the Monoforms were an attempt to make furniture without thinking about the body in any kind of detail, an exercise in removing constraints, dropping the added agenda that drives – and can sometimes overdrive – the basic reason for doing something. The Monoforms are the body-scaled version of this decoupling exercise, and Horizon is the environment-scaled

Horizon, 2007, exhibition in Rome, 2008, showing position
of Sea of Galilee image

David Adjaye: Form, Heft, Material exhibition, Munich, 2015,
with two Monoforms and the Washington Corona coffee table
on the central axis

Washington Corona coffee table, 2013

Petra Monoform, Type II, 2007

Genesis, 2011, model showing wall openings and oculus

Aïshti Foundation, Beirut, 2015, east facade

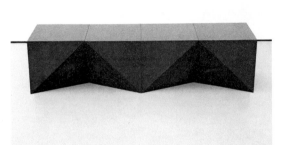

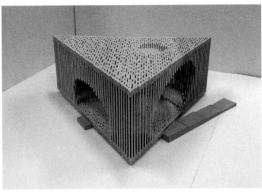

version. The freedom of the exercise is what I was looking for: the act at the scale of the object, which would give me a degree of freedom that is not permitted in other types of design project. In the Monoforms you still have the dimensions of the body in various postures, but the pragmatic details associated with conventional furniture are missing.

_The Monoforms and Horizon were partly inspired by a visit I made to desert landscapes in North Africa and the Middle East, and we included images of some of these places in the catalogue for the Albion exhibition. Their landscapes present abstract and highly visible geometries. They are landscapes where geography is expressed in clear forms, from Jordan and Petra through to the rock formations where you find citadels, such as Jerusalem. They are the alternative to the forest, which I see as nature's primary act in populating the planet. These are places where that act is resisted, and more abstract forces, like the wind, come into play. The forest can keep going, endlessly creating structures that define spaces – a system that denies form as it moves forward. But there are moments where it stumbles – a mountain or a desert – and you have fascinating abstractions. I love these deserts where the primary system is resisted and replaced by an alternative system, which is about erosion. The process of removal is central to the way I think. For me, form is excavated from complexity, and the abstraction involved in this process is a means of detaching myself from more pragmatic systems and processes. It is about searching the planet for the nature of form, rather than pursuing questions of form on a purely abstract basis. Many of the cultural artifacts that we admire from the desert region are the result of reduction. I am thinking of the Egyptian sculptures, where you can read the outline of the block from which the sculpture was carved and understand what has been taken away in the process.

_The Monoforms were conceived as a range of options that explored a limited number of fundamental questions. I was only concerned with making certain kinds of reduction, ignoring the possibility of future mutations; the Giza, Petra, Luxor and Galilee monoforms are a sort of DNA of reductions. Giza is a figure lying in the landscape, and when I say "figure," I am referring to constructed form, not the human figure. Petra is a bench, which is not a bench but a landscape that has been eroded, leaving an isolated plateau. Luxor is about forms conglomerating to create a density and a singularity, which can still be broken down into its constituent parts. Galilee represents the ultimate reduction in nature, the ultimate eroded form. Each of them had the potential to be interpreted at different scales and, as a series, they represented possibilities that I could explore in more depth at a later date. This exercise gave me a vehicle to express the intuitions that were the basis of my decision making. The Monoforms concretized these intuitions, in a process that was not a self-conscious one but came out of a period of reflection.

_The realization that a specific geometry could develop out of a landscape was very instructive because this was the time when I was struggling with the Skolkovo project on a wooded site on the outskirts of Moscow. I had never had to deal with this kind of landscape condition, and it forced me into a series of questions, at the same time as I was testing the Monoforms. My landscape buildings are never meant to be read as part of the landscape, but I always try to place the building in a position where there is a relationship between the natural and the built form. Since we completed the Skolkovo project, I have been interested in bending form, to defer to the idea of place. Our building for the Aïshti Foundation in Beirut is part of this family, and the pavilion and furniture exercises were the testing ground for this emerging area of work.

_LATER PAVILIONS

The five pavilions that I have realized since 2007 are an investigation into the hybridity of the system represented by Horizon and the Monoforms. If I was working backward to isolate primary forms in the Monoforms, what I have been exploring in the later pavilions is the hybridities – the collisions, the distortions, the mutations, the eruptions, and the disjuncture. It is a completely gripping process, which I still have to complete. The oval form and the suspended ceiling in the Sclera pavilion, for example, are derived from the Galilee monoform; Sclera shows how a system of construction can be applied to an interpretation of the form. The Genesis pavilion is the result of subtracting a dome-like space from the external form of the pavilion, which is triangular. This is the first occasion when you see a disruptive agency between the two systems, and the architecture moves forward, from playing a descriptive role to recording disruptions. Two entities come together and I cannot predict the result, which is something I observe and then take ownership of.

_When there are two entities in the later pavilions, one of them is usually represented by a void. What interests me in places like Petra is the sculptural act of removal and the resulting sense of absence. The void as a result of an action that is not about additive making is an intriguing prospect. Subtracting, rather than adding, is actually one of the most powerful acts. Creating a void in this way, the tension of the act leaves a kind of residual aura around the form, which we as humans relate to. The suspended ceiling in Sclera investigates this phenomenon; the section of the ceiling appears to be the result of cutting off and removing the hanging timbers on a programmatic basis.

_In the case of the Luxor monoform, the act of removal creates a highly ambiguous form: a tapered leaning trunk that supports a horizontal rectangular plane. I have become increasingly fascinated by the notion of the taper or the incline, which I am reading as a form that can set up relationships in many situations. It is a form that questions our expectation that the upright vertical is the primary structure. I seem to be gravitating toward this leaning gesture, this softness of form that is more accommodating to human perception. It is a device with its own perspective and is more relational than the logic of the upright. When one suggests the lean in Asian culture, it immediately connects with the vernacular architecture there, but I am not making a literal connection. My lean happens to look like the vernacular, but what I am interested in is its relevance to our contemporary condition. It can be seen as an act of defiance, without being gestural or gimmicky, and starts to distinguish between a logic based on rationality and one based on human values. It is about the idea of bringing a primal instinct back into architecture. The lean certainly creates an agelessness in the work and has the capacity to bounce past our tendency to perceive buildings as no more than the sum of their parts. I am looking at other things now, but we explored the lean in the River Reading Room in Gwangju, the Washington Corona coffee table, and the National Museum of African American History and Culture in Washington, DC.

_My motivation in pursuing the pavilion and furniture projects is to do with understanding different scales of creativity. There are many realms of creativity and I am interested in how they manifest themselves at various levels, from fabrics through to the design of buildings. These questions are not primarily to do with design but about my desire to explore all the possibilities presented by the physical world. I would be very interested in working on an issue that had no visual identity, which is probably why I am fascinated by music. In the end it is a question of what actions are possible and what they contribute to the world. When you see me shifting my attention, it is not a discourse on design but a discourse on scales of creativity. I am trying to identify the notion of the laboratory and what that might bring to the world. We are not concerned with production for its own sake, and I hope that everything we produce has a value beyond its practical purpose.

TALKING ABOUT FORM

PAVILIONS

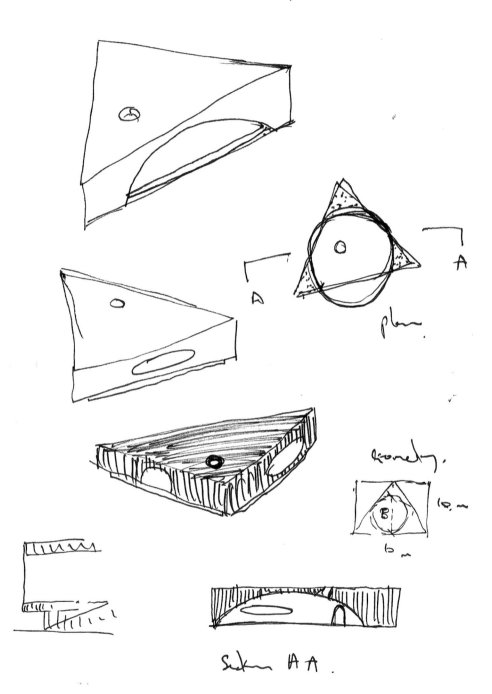

Study showing subtraction of a dome-like space from triangular solid, Genesis, 2011

Ten-meter-long wall and entrance

Two sections of the thirty-meter-long interior

Plan

Exterior

Elevation

Interior

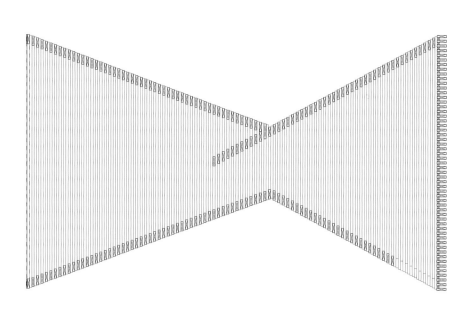

Plan

Exterior view, *David Adjaye: Form, Heft, Material* exhibition, Munich, 2015

Interior view of Sea of Galilee image, London, 2007

Interior view, *David Adjaye: Form, Heft, Material* exhibition, Munich, 2015

Model of the Monoform series

The entrance gorge, Petra, Jordan

The Obelisk Tomb, Petra, first century BCE

Giza Monoform, Type I

Luxor Monoform, Type III, 2007

Galilee Monoform, Type IV, 2007

The suspended ceiling

›

Winter view of shelter for walkers and mountain bikers

‹ Night view with the London Eye   View over high ground close to the England–Scotland border

Facade with window

A performance space for art events

A timber roof structure on diagonal concrete piers

>

HOUSES
AS SPATIAL
SYSTEMS

_SYSTEMS

When we were preparing for the exhibition of our work at the Haus der Kunst in Munich in 2015, I decided that I wanted to look at all the houses we had built as a group, which is why we presented them as a series of white models. Each of the houses is materially sensitive and has an evocative atmosphere, and all of them are designed to not let you see the system that informs their organization. They place you in an environment where you forget about the architecture, and they are successful to the point that the connections between houses are not readily apparent. By making similar white models of each one and showing them together, I was interested in revealing shared themes and connections. In all the houses there are systems in play that inform the way in which walls and windows are made, that explain the treatment of different site levels, and show how horizontality and verticality are explored. With the models, I wanted to be able to compare how these systems had operated in different locations.

_The white models decouple the houses from the material and atmospheric experience, and by showing them as solid and void abstractions, you can see how the presence of light is impacting the nature of the volumes. The windows are not being made to address the street or to express the technology of the building; they are intended to heighten the experience of living in the house. An awareness of the position of voids and solids, and how they are lit, is critical to understanding the architectural tempo of a house and how light is being used to activate and deactivate particular experiences.

_In my mind's eye the projects have no front or back, but are complete systems. This can be frustrating for clients, who do not realize how we are thinking about experience. They sometimes say, "Well, that's the back, which nobody will see; let's compromise it." My approach is not about this kind of social understanding. It is concerned with the totality of experience, and the way in which the systems that make up the house – structure, lighting, circulation, and privacy – work as a single entity, regardless of whether they are visible or hidden. In the first instance, before I think about materials, the houses are systems of abstract form and space. What these systems involve and how they relate to one another have to be sorted out before anything else can happen. When we reach that point, there can be a negotiation on the detail, but the main relationships are fixed, which is what you see in the white models.

_In my sketches I start by exploring the relationships between the main volumes, and as a composition emerges, I articulate what this means in the physical context of the site. I need to see how the systems in the house react to the situation on the site and what kind of conditions they generate. I explore this question from different angles, before moving on to articulate the architecture of the main spaces, in a process that reinforces the organizational diagram of the house. Repeating this process in quick succession, the design moves forward from one version to the next. The sketches can be quite small because they are looking at the house as a system, not as architecture.

_URBAN GRIDS

The houses are organized on an orthogonal basis for two main reasons. Until recently most of the sites have been in grid cities – cities where the streets are organized on a grid. This does not mean that the street pattern has to continue into the house but, to my mind, developing the grid is a natural choice when the geometry of the context is so clear. Secondly, when you accept the grid, trying to articulate more mutations within an existing structure is an interesting challenge. I have had to reconsider this question when we have been asked to design houses in a landscape, and my first response was to return to a rectilinear geometry by employing a scene-setting device to make a connection between the house and the landscape. In the case of Nkron, a pool defines the edge of the plinth that the main pavilion sits on; it anchors and orientates the house in the landscape. At Hill House the building plot changes direction as it moves down the hillside. This is reflected in the shape of the open courtyard, whose angled walls set up the plan of the house and the way in which the geometry works.

_The urban houses have always been in positions where they have punctuated the context, making compositions that end a sequence, articulate a change of direction, or separate one condition from another. Even though they are part of the context and not trying to fight it, using cubic forms has been instrumental in giving a certain focus to the situation. I find that cubic forms have a kind of radicality, making clear the position they occupy without being visually assertive. The models are intended to reveal this quality and show how various three-dimensional moves, which might otherwise appear to be impossible in the context, become the raison d'être of the project.

_FRAMING AND COUNTER-FRAMING

One of the things I always question in my solid-void explorations of the houses is the direction in which connections with the context are operating. It is not always about the inside going out; sometimes it involves the outside framing the inside. The window is a device that rotates between the two systems: it can be about peering out into a space or the reverse, making an external condition present in the interior. This is the function of the window at the top of the main staircase in Silverlight. It is not really a window but more a kind of mirrored frame, which uses the external view as a picture for the interior. The windows immediately below the roof of Silverlight have a similar purpose; by bringing a view of the context into the house, they complete the relationship of the interior to the exterior. Making connections of this type is about adding a further dimension to our sense of location. For me, such moves are part of a dialectic between Adolf Loos's notion of architecture, which involved framing the view, and Mies van der Rohe's concept of living directly in the context, using technology as a mediating device. I am interested in working somewhere between these positions, framing and counter-framing between these two systems.

_I have always been concerned with the roof as a horizontal elevation and this is the reason that openings in the roof – rooflights – play a significant part in the houses. This may go back to my interest in the role of atria in the houses of the ancient world but, wherever the idea came from, seeing the roof as a fifth elevation is critical. The four facades are seen from eye level, and then there is this planetary view, which is about understanding the atmosphere and elements in the vicinity of the house. It is vital for the organization of the house to acknowledge this fundamental condition and the aperture in the roof is the key device. It frames the sky and registers the light directly, rather than as a reflection on a wall or floor. Registering the light in an unfiltered way gives you a precise sense of where you are on the planet.

_THE DOUBLE ENCLOSURE

Starting with Elektra House, many of the houses are organized as a cluster of spaces standing inside a larger volume. The notion of one system operating within another system is an important architectural strategy that plays well with the complexity of the twenty-first century and the conditions we are presented with. For me, it is a basis for pursuing a certain kind of rigor in how I develop the interior, without having to express exactly what I am doing on the exterior. The gap between the interior and the exterior gives me – as the author – some relief, in reducing the obligation to impact the external world in an aggressive manner, which would be detrimental to building up successive layers of meaning. It also sets up a spatial condition that allows for special insertions on the periphery, in response to external conditions or nearby buildings.

_In the gap itself, it is possible to see the interior and the exterior as separate systems, and the vertical condition that allows me to explain how designing the building involves working through systems. The gap decouples the architecture from the functional program, bringing an element of unprogrammedness to the experience of the building. Whenever I have employed this device, clients have instinctively understood its purpose, which suggests to me that we have an emotional response when we see one system inscribed on another.

_In the urban houses there is always an external space where the systems that make the house and the conditions on the edge of the site confront each other. The inclusion of the boundary condition, which falls outside the geometry of the house, brings order face-to-face with its opposite. There is the totality of the system represented by the house, and there is the negation of the system, represented by its relationship to the residue. I am always trying to present both aspects of the system, and the negotiation between them, which is an important part of my desire not to have any hierarchy in the organizations that I am responsible for. The urban houses are about engaging with these limits: Dirty House unfolds into an intimate courtyard, whose character is defined by the context; the linear courtyard at LN House reveals the cross section of the urban block; at the bottom of the light wells in Seven, you are compressed against the rock foundations of the neighboring buildings. These moments talk about the preciousness of space and show how the residual space has an active role in relation to the form of the building.

_UNFOLDING THE SITE

Architecture is an exploration that takes place between the programmatic content of the brief and the opportunities given by the site. The boundary conditions are significant but the place where the site is located, and what you can see, are the main considerations. As you promenade through a project, the circulation system is the device that reveals these connections to the site and the context. The comparable experience in the public buildings is more emphatic, as the circulation systems in the houses can sometimes be reduced to a minimum. The organization of the circulation depends on the design strategy and the context. In cubic houses such as Elektra and Dirty, I was interested in organizing the circulation in a way that reveals the building's section, so that you know exactly where you are when you catch sight of the context. I am interested in how spaces unfold in sequence, heightening your sense of location in the process, and in creating atmospheres that support your experience and draw you through the spaces.

_The sites for some of the linear houses – Lost, LN, and Seven – were hemmed in by other buildings and part of the challenge was to find extraordinary moments in confined circumstances. Each of these houses employs courtyards, whose light draws you through the section. In Seven the vertical condition structures your experience and the horizontal movement unfolds as

HOUSES AS SPATIAL SYSTEMS

The white house models, *David Adjaye: Form, Heft, Material* exhibition, Munich, 2015

Sunken courtyard, Sunken House, London, 2003–2007

Double wall with rooflight, Elektra House, London, 1998–2000 >

Glazed wall and concrete screen, Seven, New York, 2004–2010

Framing and counter-framing, Sunken House, London, 2003–2007

a series of compressions, as you move through the vertical slices defined by the light wells. The Nanjing House is a response to an overwhelming landscape. There is a ravine on one side of the site and a view of mountains in the other direction. The design is about creating a structure that can modulate between these extraordinary moments, without being overwhelmed by them. The lighting condition constantly changes as you progress through the living space, with framed views of the landscape at key points.

_THE ROLE OF MATERIALS

The materiality of the facade plays a role in speaking to the nature of the project in its context – the materiality makes this connection. In the first place, I need a material that is capable of making an enclosure, but my concerns go further than that. The choice of material can clarify whether the project is about reclamation, a unique quality of light, a situation at the end of a garden, or whether it is the form of the house that activates the scenario. This exercise is not about wishing to achieve an effect for its own sake, or to represent the client, but is a way of talking about the urban condition, a moment in time, or the geography of the location – depending on the concerns that emerge in the project.

_If you look at the exterior of Sunken House, it has the materiality of a garden building; the timber cladding is what you might expect on a building in a landscape. The vertical boards are not part of the area's Victorian architecture but connect with the materiality of garden pavilions. This was an important distinction for me; our building avoids the masonry identity of the existing houses and, with its timber identity, inhabits the landscape. In Seven there is the notion of these monolithic concrete beams that brace the sidewalls of the neighboring buildings, concrete beams that are cut through and chopped off, to create a series of voids. The concrete is important, not as a form of exteriority but as a basis for the bracing system that identifies this project. In the case of Silverlight, the cladding is about this incredible moment of reflection on the adjacent canal, and the ability of aluminum to absorb a new luminosity.

_Most houses have a limited number of rooms, which is clear to the user. There is always a number – it can be a three-room house, a six-room house, or an eight-room house, with transitions and systems – and what fascinates me is how to make singularities and separations. The material presence of the spaces can be a way of decoupling the sense of singularity, to create a set of experiences that are framed within a larger system. In Lost House I was interested in the singularity of the living space, but I separate the bedrooms, where you have these moments that fall outside the unifying system. This kind of thinking is about exploring techniques to create one, two, three, four, five, or ten levels of complexity, and involves making complexities in the sectional organization of the house.

_When we designed Silverlight, the clients were interested in setting up a series of narratives that people would discover, depending on their relationship with the clients. They were very clear when they talked about how different people would use their house, some in a formal way and others in informal ways. My interest was in making an architectural narrative based on what you would discover if you took different routes into the house. This is why we made journeys in different materials. A singularity, employing the same materials throughout, would have said that there was no need to be intrigued by your relationship to this couple. The multiple narratives were important, but there was an additional layer of interest in overlaying the clients' agenda on a repetitive structure, a steel frame organized on a regular grid. The available space was carved up differently on each floor, and then parts of the frame were projected back into the spaces, as a kind of memory of the underlying structure. One of the surprising things about this house is that you can be on what feels like a back stair but, materially, it is extremely rich. What I am talking about here is the relationship of the clients to their own space, and the richness that making these daily journeys can give back to them.

_I am a great fan of Craig Ellwood and Pierre Koenig. Their work in California has an economy of structure – a postwar economy – and an incredible emotive power. When you look at the Eames House, their ability to use very little material to evoke an emotional context is inspirational. In terms of the emotional quality of the architecture, the Case Study Houses exemplified the use of the minimum materials for the maximum impact. Everything about them, including the landscape, was directed to that end – in Pierre Koenig's work, for example he uses the lushness of the landscape to monumentalize the architecture. Since then the reduction in the use of material that this postwar generation searched for has become generalized and created a situation where the emotional relationship that we used to have with load-bearing structures is now lost. The Case Study Houses and Mies van der Rohe's work in Chicago sum up that development and suggest a new approach to structure and the use of materials.

_I have learnt these lessons but realize that we are not facing a *tabula rasa*. In my work materials are deployed for their ability to create emotional conditions – unique conditions – without needing to refer to the load-bearing aesthetic associated with masonry construction. In exploring what these materials are capable of, I oscillate between a desire to create enclosure – and to find systems that create enclosure – and an interest in using materials to emanate atmospheres. As the models show, this hybridized approach to materials and structure allows me to make smooth transitions between building elements with very different functions.

_EXCLUSIVE AND INCLUSIVE TRAJECTORIES

The houses and the public buildings are two facets of my output, but there is no formal connection between them – apart from being by the same author. Sometimes people have said that the houses look more hermetic but that is not really the point. The houses have a privileging trajectory while the public buildings invite you in – these two building types are about different worlds. When I make a house, I never make an inclusive trajectory; they are always houses for particular people, and the design reflects their relationship to others, and to the context. In the public buildings there is a deep agenda involving forms of organization that have a high degree of redundancy built into them, to allow for the maximum degree of inclusion. If you make a public building that is privileging, you are saying that it is for people with a certain kind of knowledge, and I find this fundamentally problematic. The unfolding of space in the houses can be very intimate while the public buildings need to offer a range of options, to address the greatest diversity. The public buildings are about fighting for redundancy, as a way to generate clarity.

HOUSES

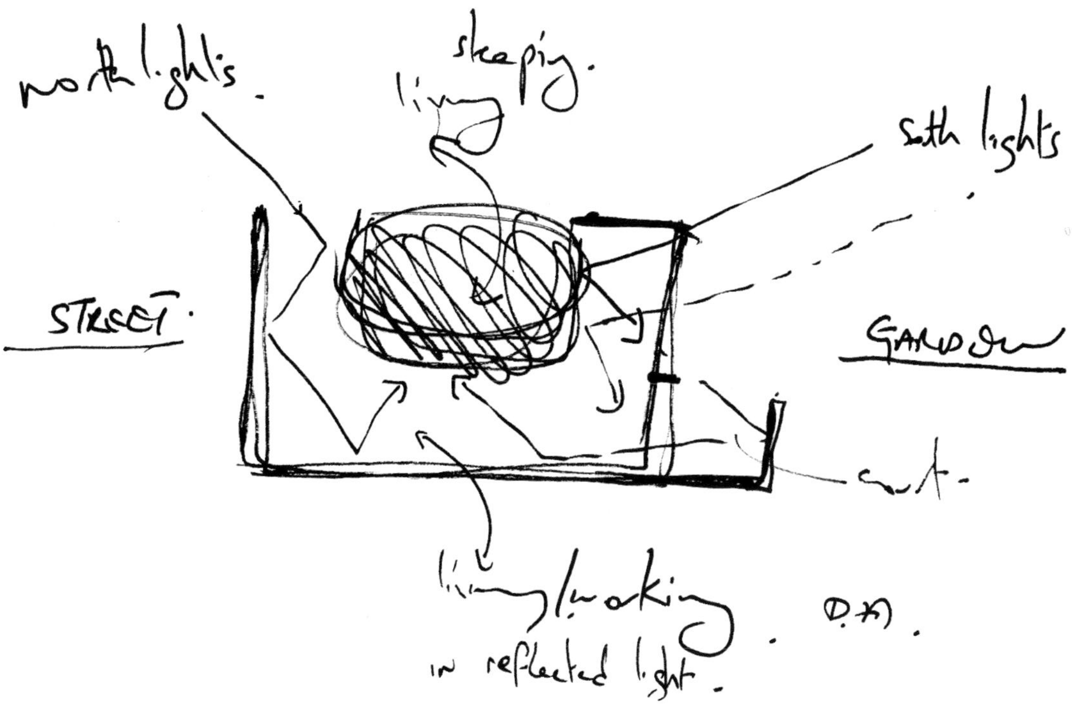
north lights.
sleeping.
living
south lights
STREET.
GARDEN
court.
living/working
in reflected light.
D.A.

Study section for Elektra House, London, 1998–2000

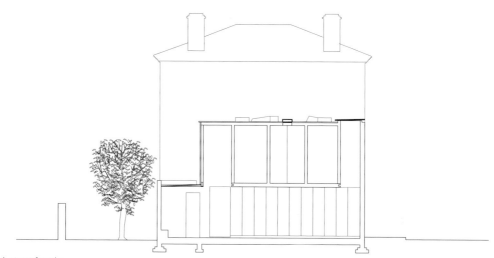

White model, street facade

White model, rear facade and courtyard   Section

Street view showing house on the right

Living space

Interior view of courtyard facade

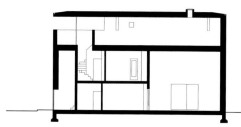

White model, street facade and position of courtyard   Section

Facade with anti-vandal paint

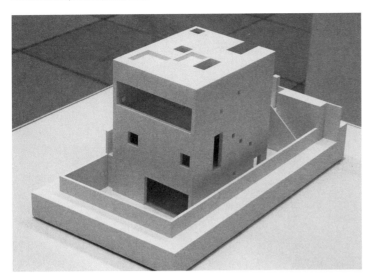

White model, side and rear facades, and courtyard

Section

Front facade with timber cladding

White model with sidewall removed

Street view showing screen to courtyard

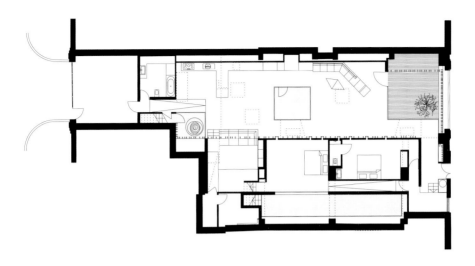

Plan showing three courtyards (above) and lap pool (below)

Bedroom with window to glazed court

Living space looking toward street

White model, section and rear facade

Street facade

Entrance space

Back stair with Zebrano lining

Main stair with lightweight concrete wall panels

Master bedroom, second floor

Window with mirrored frame

Living space, third floor

South facade overlooking canal

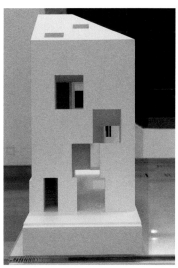

White model, section

White model, street facade

Street view showing screen-printed polypropylene cladding

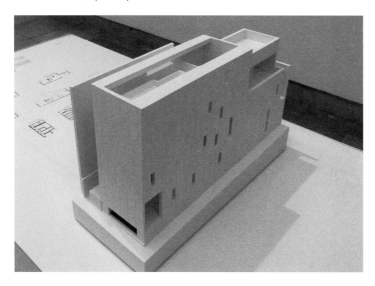

White model, front and side facades, and roof deck

Street view showing Corten steel cladding

Glazed court (left), third floor

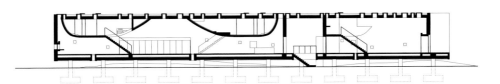

White model, front and end facades   Section

Living space with curved ceiling

White model, historic front facade and section

Central void

View across central court from living space, second floor

Entrance to gallery space, ground floor

Light well and schist foundations

White model, guest pavilions (left) and main house (right)

Cantilevered roof, guest pavilion

Pigmented concrete, main house

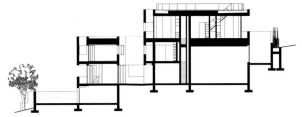

White model, stepped volumes

Section

Street view

MATT AND SHEEN, MATERIAL STRATEGIES 1996–2016

_RESIGNIFICATION

The resignification of materials is an idea that came up when I was looking for a conceptual methodology for the work we were doing in the 1990s, which often involved interventions in existing buildings. I was not particularly interested in responding to each of the situations we were presented with on a one-off basis. Taking a broader view, these projects presented an opportunity to think about the overall significance and meaning of this type of interior work. In changing the use and the ambience of existing spaces, the selection and detailing of materials played a major role and, for us, there were two main options: using old materials in new ways or, alternatively, new materials in a way that would give them an air of familiarity. This gave us an initial set of fascinating experiments. If you look at Soba, Lunch, and the Social, they were all about reappropriating industrial materials in small-scale commercial projects. Occasionally, we used old materials, such as oak, in settings that were entirely contemporary. We were attempting to use a diversity of materials in a principled way, to signify spatial experience. The aim was to generate an alphabet of primary relationships, using double-height and tubular spaces to set up served and subservient spaces.

_I was primarily interested in a language of form-making – form as space, form as presence-making, form as a way of making things present in the here and now. Materials do not simply operate on their own account; the context in which you place them informs how they read. Both aspects need to work together to reveal the overall orientation of the project. In the noodle restaurant Soba, our idea was to treat the space as an alleyway between two buildings, to give people the idea that they were sitting down in the city – rather than in a room in the city. We treated the internal walls as if they were facades of buildings standing on the alley, to give a sense of exteriority. It was quite Palladian in representing the exterior on the interior – as Palladio did at the Villa Malcontenta, which has views of the gardens painted on the internal walls. When you sit in the villa's living room you think you are in the garden, but you are surrounded by all the other rooms in the house. In our projects we were taking spaces that came with a history and reprogramming them with a different spatial narrative. In making interiors as exteriors, we were also referring to the role of unformed spaces in the city, the residual spaces between buildings that are not deliberately formed but have this wonderful quality and power.

_Working in confined spaces, we sometimes made moves to undermine the apparent solidity of walls. On the lower floor of The Social, a bar in central London, the sidewalls are lined with backlit GRP (glass reinforced plastic) and glow with light, while the tables and seating are in cast concrete, to give a sense of physical location. At the fashion store Browns Focus, we used the central staircase constructed in recycled timber as the physical anchor. Lining the space with mirrors and translucent glass, we tried to completely dissolve the perimeter enclosure, and the stair was the device that organizes what happens within the dissolved condition. There were multiple spatial possibilities, all of which could be accessed from the stair; the limits of the project were the perimeter and the stair, and anything was possible between them. Projects such as Browns, and our installations at the Selfridges department store, represent the unfolding of a discussion about reflective surfaces and how they allowed us to extend the depth of a space when we were unable to make a physical subtraction from the structure. Whenever we needed to make a subtraction that could not be realized in any other way, we made the shift to reflective surfaces. These projects were about narratives of space and how they could be deconstructed, or remade and reimagined, through the action of material choice. In the Luxury Plaza at the Selfridges store in London, the anchor was the central space. Although it had reflecting surfaces, we saw this space as a civic plaza – a metaphysical square.

_Resignification also played a part in the development of the Elektra House. It was originally designed as a double-datum building, with a paneled system at ground level and a glazed reflective system on the floor above. As part of a matt-and-sheen strategy, areas of translucent glazing would have been punctuated by occasional windows, framing reflections of the sky when seen from outside. We reached a point where the clients could not afford to follow through on this strategy, so we moved to an approach that I had been working on in the studio. The idea was to make a monolithic structure in which the materiality of a familiar material would be presented in a way that was unfamiliar. At the time we were using phenolic plywood to make the shuttering for casting concrete, and I was fascinated by its visual qualities, as well as its physical performance. With its appearance and strength in mind, I began to move away from a facade that would continue the articulation of the existing street, toward one that would blank the street, as though it were a building-size blank window or a gable wall – which is not really a facade at all. I did not want my building to be part of the Victorian terrace or a continuation of the existing streetscape, and this industrial material – the phenolic plywood – allowed me to close down the expression of the street facade. I was then free to focus on the roof and the back of the house, which is where we had the light and the views. The economic condition presented by the clients allowed me to clarify my position, which was about understanding the street on a more conceptual basis. From the blind frontage on the street, the internal organization moves from the spaces lit by rooflights to the back facade, which opens up to the sky and a small courtyard.

_THE MATERIAL TABLE AND MAKING PUBLIC BUILDINGS

After the completion of Elektra, we moved to larger offices on Penn Street in the North Hoxton area of London, where there was space to display a full range of materials. We placed multiple samples of different types of material on trays and assembled them on a long bench, down one side of a passage that led from the reception area to the conference space. This arrangement was the basis for the Material Table, the system I developed for selecting the combinations of materials that you see in our first public buildings. These projects were won in competition over a relatively short period of time, and they overlapped with each other in terms of their requirements and the roles they were expected to play in the city. As designs, they unfolded as a family of types, which is how I presented them in the *Making Public Buildings* exhibition at the Whitechapel Gallery in 2006. This was the idea behind the cover of the exhibition catalogue; the sketch we used was about laying out the architectural types that these buildings allowed me to explore. There were many other ways to approach the design of the public buildings in London, but a spectral strategy was the normal choice for me. Along with thinking about architectural types, it seemed inevitable that materials would play a significant role in the specificity of each building. With the options laid out in the Material Table as the starting point, we were interested in developing a material language that could engage with specific situations and, at a later stage, would connect one project with another. Our aim was to explore a diversity of systems that had common roots, one of which was the Material Table.

– Our first commission for a public building was the Nobel Peace Center in Oslo, and it involved recycling a historic building; in this respect there was an overlap with the interior projects of the 1990s. The center would need to have an identity of its own, but this could only be achieved through working with the existing building. Fortunately, the notion of using material and form to create the new experience – the presence of experience – had been rehearsed in many small projects and houses by the time we started to develop the center. The design challenge was to do with maintaining continuity in a narrative that had to be organized across a large diversity of rooms. As we were unable to reconfigure the structure, we employed a particular range of materials to create that powerful presence within the existing building. The key spaces are the reception area, finished in red resin, the Passage of Honor, lined in brass to commemorate the current laureate, the Nobel Field, where the work of previous laureates is celebrated in an interactive display recalling flowers in a landscape, and the Café de la Paix where the green mural by Chris Ofili represents the world at peace. These interventions pushed the existing architecture into the background, except when we use it to frame a view or give a sense of scale.

– The first major new build project was the Idea Store Whitechapel, where I was interested in the Victorian context and how it might relate to a contemporary institution. There was nothing literal about my interest in the surrounding fabric; I was simply fascinated by the lines that make form. On Whitechapel Road, where our building stands, the facades are inscribed with a series of horizontals, Victorian strata that developed the cross section of the city. Then there are the vertical lines that relate to party walls and establish the widths of facades and the gaps between buildings. We had decided on a glass building, as a deliberate counter to the brick and occasional stone details of the area's commercial and residential architecture. The idea was to use material to codify difference. Where the context was opaque, we were transparent, and vice-versa – making a translucent or transparent building on an opaque street would signal publicness. But rather than using the metrics of high-tech architecture, which talks about the dimensions of industrial production, we connected with this contextual system of lines, which establish horizontal and vertical relationships and suggested an interesting basis for connecting our project with the surrounding buildings. You have an abstract representation of what I am talking about on the external facade of the Idea Store Whitechapel and a more physical expression on the inside. Within this scaffold, there are various subsets of materials that develop the narrative of the project. The idea of paper, wood, and fiber being part of the same manufacturing process makes a connection with books. To highlight this theme, there are moments where we use the opposite type: crystalline materials, such as the aluminum cladding on the lift and staircase core, or recyclable materials, like the rubber flooring.

_There are some London projects that do not have a material density and employ a narrower range of materials. Their materiality is about the coloration of light, which is connected with the tonal presence of the building and its ability to amplify local conditions. In the Bernie Grant Arts Centre, there was an idea of these amplified moments of tonality that would rhyme or contrast with nearby buildings, whether they were part of our project or on adjacent sites. The center is a campus in its own right and is also part of a larger campus of historic buildings. We used materiality and color to talk about the development of our site as a single construction, and to make connections between buildings. The color and tone of each building set up a series of shifting relationships, moving across the site, and into and out of buildings. The dark-brown cladding on the sidewalls of the Auditorium building, for example, matches the color of the Purpleheart timber that we used for the walls and ceiling of the foyer, which leads into the auditorium space with its deep-red walls. In general, we employed materiality and color to make connections with the context and to develop the roles of the different buildings.

–In the Stephen Lawrence Centre and the Museum of Contemporary Art Denver (MCAD), the facades are not about physicality; they are systems that are purely about drawing a certain kind of light. The cladding of the Stephen Lawrence building is expanded metal mesh, which picks up the dappled light from the foliage of the trees and from the surface of the river that runs along one edge of the site. Developing the strategy we had followed in the interior projects that employed reflecting surfaces, the Stephen Lawrence building has a floating presence in the landscape setting, while the internal spaces are completely unambiguous in their materiality and use of color. In the MCAD the facade filters the light as it passes into the building, reflecting some of it outward in the process. This double action accounts for the weightless quality of the exterior, while the cross-shaped space, which cuts through the center of the building, anchors the building in the city. In terms of their color and texture, the materials we used here do not have an emphatic presence, as they are required to work together to subdue the light to begin with, and then enhance what remains of it. The narrative in these buildings comes from drawing with light, rather than material representation.

–The materiality of the Rivington Place and Stephen Lawrence buildings may look very different, but in my mind they are two sides of the same coin. This was the question we explored in the two libraries we designed in Washington, DC. The site of the Francis A. Gregory Library is not dissimilar to that of the Stephen Lawrence Centre. It is a building in a forest and the

Soba, London, 1996

Sugar Hill, New York, 2011–2014, entrance detail

Aïshti Foundation, Beirut, Lebanon, 2012–2015, atrium

slatted roof and the reflective facades amplify the tonality of the trees. As in the London building, the materiality of the interior is very precise. Each element of the library takes on an appropriate physical definition: the double-height Teen Services space, the facetted glass walls of the Adult Learning space, the curving timber screen of the Children's Program room, and so on. They reveal different aspects of the library's program and are held together by the diagonal pattern of the Douglas Fir plywood panels on the inside faces of each facade. In the same section of the city, the William O. Lockridge Library occupies a sloping site, which is one block from a main thoroughfare and surrounded by single-family houses. Reflecting local typologies, the facades of this building are regular solid-void compositions that protect the interior and, from the inside, open up to views of the surroundings. The materiality of the larger internal spaces, on the other hand, plays the demateriality of reflective surfaces against the solidity of the structure.

_ATMOSPHERES

In all of the examples I have discussed, there was a broad strategic decision on materiality, but the real work was in selecting the combinations of materials that would fine-tune the strategy to the program and the context. By categorizing materials according to their physical and visual properties in a continuous scale of options, the Material Table is a useful tool at both stages. During the period when we were developing the public buildings in London, I was working on Silverlight, a house that explored a wide range of material combinations. Standing between a busy road and a canal in west London, Silverlight has a steel frame that is four bays wide, and cantilevers toward the front and rear of the house. The frame is the organizing element of the entire project but is inhabited by a number of events, spatial sequences where the materials codify and lead you through a series of narratives.

_Little of this is visible from the outside, which is clad in a system of aluminum panels. The street-level entrance slides open to reveal a red resin-finished carport and a cross wall coated in crushed glass, which directs you to the front door. There is no natural light in the entrance space and the walls are clad in a dark shade of Polyrey plastic. This is a pause space to assess the circulation options: a Zebrano-clad "back" stair leading to the floors above, a continuous concrete staircase taking you directly to the top-floor living room, or a short passage leading to the guest bedrooms, whose ceilings are the exposed steel shuttering for the concrete floor above. The first stop on the back staircase is the master-bedroom suite, where sections of the walls are clad in bamboo and layered crushed glass, with Zebrano used for the sleeping dais. These spaces open directly into a sand-resin-finished courtyard. Reversing the section of a London terrace house, both staircases terminate in the top-floor living space, with its polished concrete floor, aluminum-clad walls, and concrete sofa. None of the material combinations in the house has the singularity to explain the system behind the building; that is the role of the structure, which is revealed throughout the project. Due to their relative independence, we were able to fine-tune the material combinations in each zone of the house to create a series of distinctive atmospheres.

_MATERIAL STRATEGIES

In residential architecture the distinction between the interior and the exterior – and the notion of the curated interior – seem to be connected with northern climates; the difference between inside and outside does not register in the same way in southern climates. In the house we built in Ghana and in Hill House in Trinidad, the interior is a continuation of the exterior. There are material moments in both of these houses, but basically they use the same construction for the interior and the exterior. Our recent public buildings, in northern and southern climates, maintain the inside-outside distinction and, unlike the first generation of public buildings, often employ several material strategies in parallel. In the Sugar Hill building there is a strategy to do with each of the main elements. The early childhood center at street level has the most open relationship to the outside – to the internal courtyard or the external view – and the teaching spaces are designed around this inside-outside dissolve. At the lower level, the gallery spaces in the Children's Museum of Art and Storytelling are more self-contained but connected to the outside by a long rooflight that makes a channel of light through the plan. The apartments in the shaft of the building pick up on the condition of residential architecture in New York, and the pigmented concrete panels and the incised rose motif reference Harlem's brownstone buildings.

_There is a similar tripartite division in the National Museum of African American History and Culture. Sixty feet below street level, the History Galleries are the foundation of the institution and are housed in a crypt-like space in raw concrete: a monolithic chamber that, with its exhibits, becomes a cave of wonder. Above ground, the Corona is organized as a neutral enclosure, which houses exhibition spaces, a library, education rooms, and offices, behind a more expressive facade system. At ground level, Heritage Hall stands between the History Galleries and the Corona; it is the arrival space, a place of celebration, and a new urban room for the city. The experience at every level is conditioned by having already seen the bronze finish facades of the Corona, and we have reinforced this connection in the materiality of the interior. The metal-working theme is continued in the sheet-steel ceiling of Heritage Hall, in the Corten steel Monumental Stair that connects the hall to the crypt, and in the copper system that we use to clad the structural piers that support the Corona. In the main auditorium, the upper sections of the walls consist of a smaller-scale version of the abstract plant-based pattern employed on the facade, executed in fibrous cement.

_I would like to conclude by looking at the Aïshti Foundation building in Beirut. This is a hybrid building with two main functions: it extends the client's shopping complex at the southern end of the site and includes a separate art gallery to house his collection of contemporary art. The site is located between the coastal highway and the Mediterranean, and the client was interested in creating a public landscaped space between the new building and the sea. From the beginning, my aim was to celebrate these different programmatic conditions with a narrative about form making and atmosphere. The

Aïshti building is the first test of this approach. In the museum section you have load-bearing walls that are expressed in single- and double-height volumes – chambers and viewing galleries, as an expression of a museum. At the other end of the building, you have the interiority of the shopping experience, which is about the gaze and seeing things obliquely. The funnel-shaped atrium is supposed to be a space without direct sunlight, but it is actually completely drenched in daylight, which is reflected with so much artificial light that you cannot tell which is which. Both narratives – the museum and the shopping experience – take place in close proximity and, although it is possible to move between them, there is no connecting threshold, no respite space inside the building where you have relief from them. These two immersive environments are experientially very different but exist side by side in one building – that is the innovation. They are protected from the sun and from traffic noise by a double facade whose external skin is an aluminum lattice. The finish on the aluminum is the same color as the city's traditional tile roofs and the pattern of the facade represents waves approaching the shore.

MATT AND SHEEN,
MATERIAL STRATEGIES 1996–2016

MAKING PUBLIC BUILDINGS

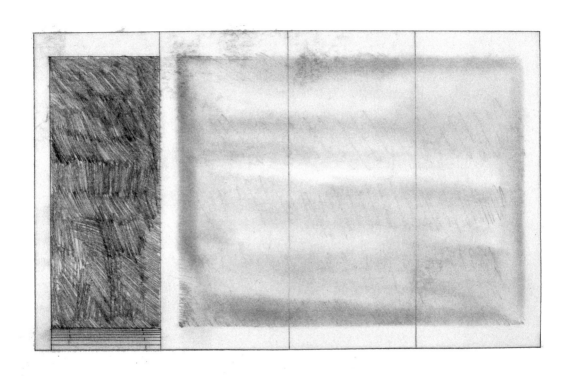

FRONT ELEVATION 1:20 ASYMETRK CHAMBER DAVID ASTATE 8/7/2003

Oak-lined bar

Concrete furniture and illuminated wall

Browns Focus, London, 2001, recycled timber staircase with reflective walls and ceiling

Selfridges Luxury Plaza, London, 2003

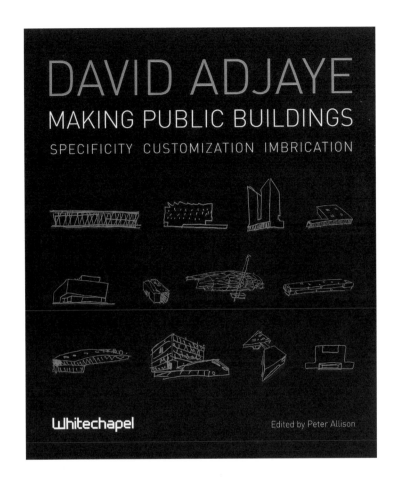

Book cover, *David Adjaye: Making Public Buildings*, London, 2006

‹ The materials table, Penn Street office, London

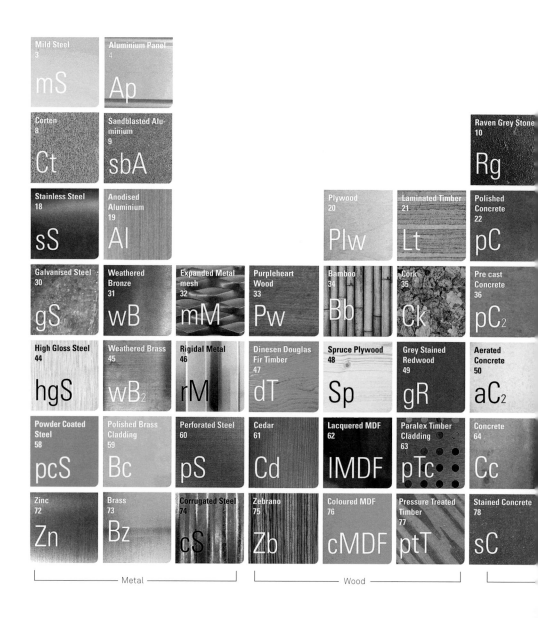

The Material Table, showing the project materials employed between 2002 and 2009,
in *Material Table* exhibition catalogue, London, 2011

						Polyrey Plastic 1 prP	Polycarbonate 2 Pl
				Layered Crushed Glass 5 lcG	GRP 6 Grp		Recycled Plastic Panels 7 rP
Black Stained Brick 11 oB	Terazzo 12 Tz	Felt 13 Ft	Coloured Glass Interlayer 14 cG	Back Painted Glass 15 Bp	Red Resin 16 Rr		Translucent Polycarbonate 17 tP
Splitface Block 23 Sb	Stone 24 St	Polyester 25 Py	Grey Glass 26 gG	Transparent Glass 27 tG	Blue Rubber flooring 28 Br		Monopan 29 Mp
Grey Slate 37 Gs	Pebbles 38 Ps	Wool 39 W	Laminate Green Glass 40 lgG	Opaque Glass 41 oG	Green Rubber flooring 42 Gr		Rubber Mat 43 Rm
Sienna Slate 51 sS₂	Ceramic 52 Ce	Leather 53 L	Laminate Blue Glass 54 lbG	Translucent Glass 55 tG₂	Norament Rubber Flooring 56 Nr		Mastic Asphalt 57 Ma
Grey/Green slate 65 gS₂	Porcelian 66 Pc	Carpet 67 Ca	Laminated Clear Glass 68 lcG	Toughened Glass 69 tG₃	Black Rubber Flooring 70 Ru		Recycled Tortoise Shell 71 Ts
Stained Plaster 79 sP	Clay Tiles 80 Cti	Kvadrate Soft Cell 81 Ksc	Gradient Coloured Glass 82 gcG	Mirror Glass 83 Mi	Perspex 84 Px		PVDF Plastic 85 PVDF

— Stone — — Fabric — — Glass — — Plastic —

| Glass Panels by Chris Ofili 86 Gco | Resin Flooring 87 Rf | Aluminium Foam Laminated Glass 88 Alg | Aluminium Honeycomb 89 Alh | Fibre Reinforced Concrete 90 Tc | Wood Wool 91 Ww | Laminated Veneer Lumber 92 lV |
| Sand Resin 93 Sr | Aluminium & Resin 94 Alr | Crushed Glass Resin 95 cG₂ | Zebrano Veneer 96 Zv | Wood Fibre board 97 Wf | Bear grass 98 Bg | Orientated Strandboard 99 Osb |

— Composite Materials —

The refurbished facades of old Vestbanen station   Café de la Paix

Reception space

Passage of Honor

The Nobel Field

South facade

Suspended atrium with market stalls

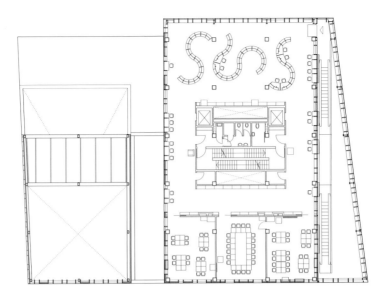

Plan, third floor

Library space, third floor

Model showing main floor

Street view showing how the upper story stands on an existing concrete deck (left and right)

Gallery space looking toward the street

Street view looking towards Shoreditch Town Hall

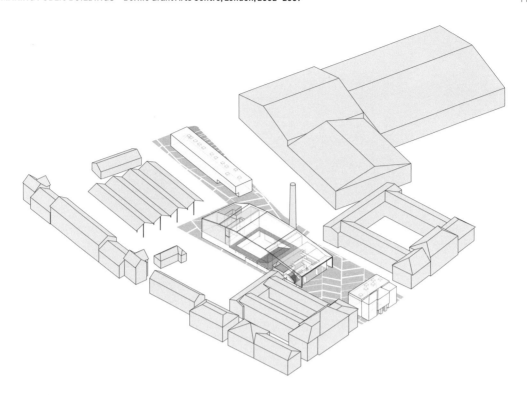

Isometric drawing with Hub (right), Auditorium (center),
and Enterprise Building (left)

Auditorium, front facade with reflection of the Hub   Auditorium, foyer with Purpleheart timber lining   >

Auditorium space

The Hub, seen from the Auditorium

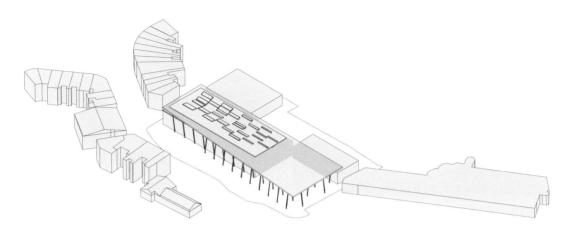

Isometric drawing showing the existing buildings and bus station (right)

View from bus station forecourt

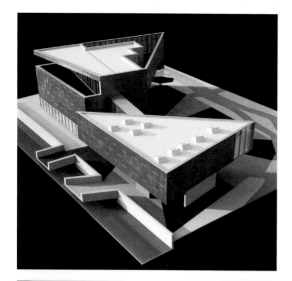

Model, river facade

Studio space

Lobby

Street view showing position of lobby (right)

Lobby window designed by Chris Ofili

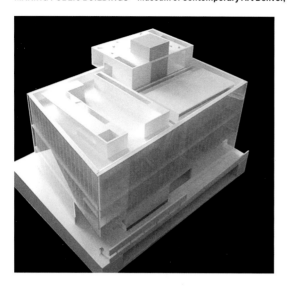

Model showing roof deck

East facade showing corner entrance

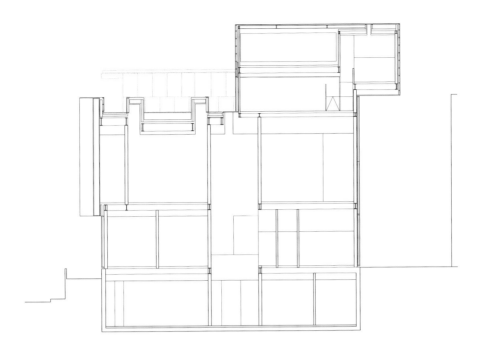

Section

Perimeter passage and gallery, second floor

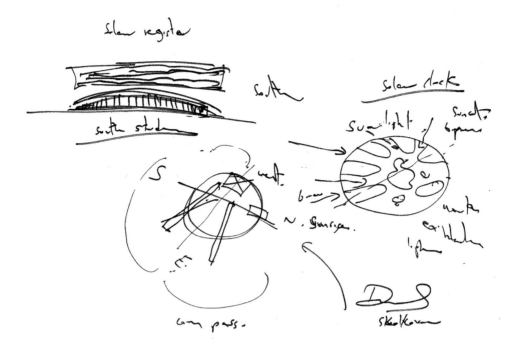

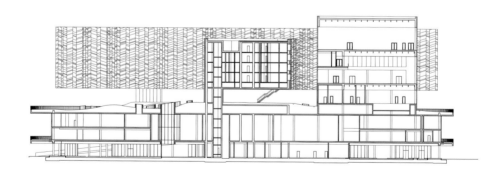

Studies of the Disc and superstructure

Section through the Disc, the Administration Tower (center), and the Wellness Center (right)

The Disc and cantilevered residential buildings (left)

Winter view showing position in landscape

LIGHT AND THE CITY

_PLACE

My buildings are intended to be open to engagement; this was a deliberate strategy from the day that I designed the Elektra House. The design of Elektra was a critique of the Victorian street and its insistence on a certain kind of formality, which was intended to support public life – while the back facades of the houses were completely informal. The historic context was an issue in this project because I believed that the previous formality was no longer an accurate reflection of the society that we live in, and that the schizophrenia that it represented had to be reversed. Creating an architecture that had an explicit relationship with the experience of being in the city was very important to me. The historic link between the history of the city and the facades of its buildings, which may previously have been necessary as part of organizing a civil society, struck me as no longer relevant to the experience of contemporary life.

_I see my creativity as centered in the analysis of place, as a means of establishing the relevance of the project. This desire may come from an inability I have to create things that are self-contained. The city is always evolving and this is how we need to understand it, rather than seeing it as an impersonal system. What is particularly interesting about the European city at the moment is that it has arrived at a critical point where we need to investigate a new kind of density, a social and cultural density rather than one based on numerical addition. For this reason, I am interested in projects that form an intimate connection between the individual and the city, projects that encourage people to identify with the life of the city. The disconnect between the object and the person needs to be reversed and replaced by a closer sense of engagement.

_I am concerned with people's experience, rather than with structures of authority. The way that I approach the question of experience is by closely observing the conditions in a place before I start work. Often there are several interests at play, and by making connections between them, they take on a heightened identity. In this sense, many of my projects can be seen not as self-contained buildings but as pieces of the city, housing a variety of activities in a range of spaces. They combine the impersonality of the city with an identity that results from the persistence of certain uses over time. The Elektra House is a good example; it is very small but includes a wide range of spaces, especially when you include the entrance sequence. Although it is only a house, it is like being in the city in terms of the range of spatial experience it provides.

_THE CITY

The idea of the city and the richness of city experience always give the most important clue, in terms of how I establish the spatial construction of a project. This is nothing to do with the sum of the constructional possibilities but is a kind of synthesis of the spatial narrative that informs the reality of a particular place. Whether a project is large or small, the idea of making a microcosm of the city is a great stimulus. I firmly believe that the richness of the city comes from its exteriority, rather than its interiority. My aim is to magnify this exteriority as an interior phenomenon – banning the conventional notion of the interior and replacing it with an interiority based on continuing the spatial pattern of the city.

_Abstraction is the tool that I use to unify the different areas of concern that arise during the development of a project, but it is not a neutral abstraction. There is often a tension between the needs of the present and the promise of the future, but they are not necessarily in conflict. For me, they potentialize the project, and the existence of a possible disconnect provides the framework to open up a new kind of experience within the strategy. The external envelope and the physical profile of a building are an opportunity to summarize what the strategy is about, and to invent a new silhouette within the composition of the city that speaks of the conditionality of a particular time. At the Idea Store Whitechapel, for example, I was interested in the unresolved nature of rupturing the building by making the cantilevered cavity – the suspended atrium – on the front facade. In terms of the visual implications involved, the structure supporting the cantilever is not resolved because the meter-deep beams on the roof appear to make reference to the external roof beams in Mies van der Rohe's work, but he never constructed a wall that did not make contact with the ground. It is a reference that is contradicted, and as a result of this ambiguity, the facade can be read in several different ways.

_ENCLOSURE

In talking about this idea of enclosure, I am concerned about its meaning in relation to both the city and the interior. The spatial phenomenon of the interior does give clues about how to handle the enclosure but without being emphatic. In the Rivington Place building there is a sequence of spaces in the body of the building, and there is another narrative that plays out on the roof. This is when I first understood how the detailed reading of a building's profile could change its overall presence. I am referring to the impact of the shed roof, which appears to deny normal perspective. The sequence of internal spaces and the external profile come together in a single statement that is legible at street level. The shed roof refers to the industrial heritage of the area and, at the same time, speaks about the notion of art spaces and visual perception – about interactive spaces that open up in sequence as one moves through them.
_In focusing on the external silhouette of my buildings, I am interested in achieving a certain kind of scalelessness, without denying the basic dimensions of the structure. But the representation of structure is more complicated than simply restating the platonic diagrams that have become all pervasive; structure is a complex phenomenon that needs to be understood as an experience, not just as a signifier. When it comes to the skin, I try to avoid a dominant reading based on a particular scale, because this gives me the freedom to adjust the perception of the architecture in relation to its position in the city. Despite my concern for context, I do not want to be limited by the particularity of the existing situation and I want to avoid anything that smacks of mimicry. Because I am interested in what architecture can offer the city in conditions that are already very dense, I need a way of establishing a degree of maneuverability in situations that are approaching overload.
_Another aspect of enclosure concerns the pattern of the cladding materials, whether it is at the scale of the Elektra House

< Central space, Museum of Contemporary Art Denver,
Denver, 2004–2007

Upper level of foyer, Auditorium, Bernie Grant Arts Centre,
London, 2002–2007

View from the Disc, Moscow School of Management Skolkovo,
Moscow, 2006–2010

Facade patterns, Moscow School of Management Skolkovo,
Moscow, 2006–2010

North facade, National Museum of African American History
and Culture, Washington, DC, 2009–2016

or the Moscow School of Management Skolkovo. The strength of the pattern is something that needs to be carefully controlled. It can be very restrained and require close observation, like Elektra, or it can be bold and extrovert, as in the case of the Skolkovo building. This is to do with the context. Compared with working in the inner city, the suburban site of the Skolkovo building lacked physical density and was an opportunity to make the appearance of the building more intense. The facades of the Museum of Contemporary Art Denver (MCAD) were designed to anticipate the other developments that have since occurred in that area. There is now a massive tower right in front of the building, which I knew was coming, and the completion of the urban condition intensifies the experience of the museum building. It is very soft in appearance because that is how I wanted to code the idea of an art institution which is not in competition with the commercial and residential architecture that now surrounds it.

_I see the patterned silhouette as having the potential to refer to the present whilst suggesting the future. It can be emphatic and recessive at the same time, inviting the observer to project their own expectations onto it, to compensate for any gaps in their understanding. Here again, I am trying to engage people on the basis of their experience, and they have to look for clues. The building does not provide a complete system of signs that speaks about the function of the building and how you should proceed. It is meant to offer a wider sense of engagement. I am concerned that as many people as possible should be able to relate to what they see, and if I were to invent a complete system, it might exclude people who could not understand what it was about. In that case, people would be put in a position where they had to accept the totality of the building or decide to have nothing to do with it.

_INTERIOR TYPOLOGIES

I do not wish to privilege the first perception of the building and force the viewer to engage with it. I feel that an inviting interior should be the final reward for being drawn to a building. This is analogous to the type of civic society that we have now, where it is less about the dress that you wear and more about the person you are. In terms of strategy, my buildings tend to unfold slowly toward the core, rather than revealing everything at once. Even when the buildings are bold on the outside, there is still a sense of them unfolding. In the Moscow School of Management Skolkovo, which probably has the boldest exterior, there is a surprising degree of richness when you come to the interior with its scalloped spaces. Although you have that boldness due to being in a suburban landscape, the underlying intention is that you should be drawn slowly toward the center.

_If the exteriors of my buildings are open to several possible readings, the interiors are intended to support all the activities that are part of the building's program. They do not offer a single perception but require detailed exploration in some sort of sequential manner. You only understand what they have to offer when you have completed that process, so they are not like a traditional public building where you expect to see the position of the main spaces, and the relationship between them, as soon as you enter. At the Stephen Lawrence Centre, you need to see everything to understand the totality, but you do not have to complete the story on a single occasion. It is supposed to reveal its sequences as you use it over time.

_The relationship between inside and outside brings up the question of iconography. While the exterior, the traditional carrier of meaning, is relatively mute in my work, the key interiors often make direct reference to elements of the city: a street market, in the Idea Stores; the steps of a major public building, in the foyer of the Auditorium at the Bernie Grant Arts Centre; the streetscape of historic Denver, in the MCAD; the interior of an airport, in the Skolkovo building, and so on. For me, this is part of a need to work in the spatial language that is present in the project's background. I do not intend to be patronizing or simplistic, but I am interested in the reuse of language and the shifts of meaning when things are repositioned. This gives the interiors of my buildings a certain familiarity, side by side with a new kind of phenomenology. It is a language of place, rather than a self-contained language of architecture – it becomes architectural but that is not the starting point.

_A good example is the foyer of the Auditorium building at the Bernie Grant Centre, which is the most important space in the project, apart from the auditorium. The program for the center anticipated that, on completion, it would provide a natural focus for the local community, but, due to the constraints of the site, the foyer is difficult to see from the nearest road. To address the expectations in the brief and the conditions on the ground, the change in level that is required to access the upper level of the auditorium has been organized as a cluster of staircases and ramps, with many opportunities to linger and take in the wider situation. This arrangement mirrors the changes in level that are often found around historic public buildings. The grandeur of this memorial project is manifest as an interior at the focal point of the site – without this space, the project would collapse. The interconnected levels are a response to the requirements in the brief, realized within a framework of memories of other locations. I believe in making references, but ambient memory has more power over our intuition, and too much specificity of detail would endanger that.

_The most explicitly urban interior is that of the MCAD. Where the building stands was part of Denver's historic downtown. Once inside, you are surrounded by these building-like volumes, creating a pedestrian environment that is reminiscent of the old city. This is very deliberate. In the United States the city is a matrix of super-functional systems for getting from A to B, and the experience of the human in the city has become a secondary consideration. The sense of planning, the sense of efficiency, and the sense of infrastructure are what organize the American city. I wanted to revive the idea of the city as a place for people. I am always playing with these apparent contradictions, in this case between the interior and exterior scenography. The facades are a response to contemporary Denver, while the interior presents an abstraction of historic Denver. For me, the business of viewing art is scientific and systematic, but also quite romantic – it requires a belief in a whole catalogue of things. The interior of the museum proposes a slightly fantastic version of the city, an ideal city that is based on the human body in space.

_LIGHT

In seeking to address different conditions on the outside and the inside of my buildings, light plays an important role. The exterior deflects attention to the context; the color can be recessive, shadowy, dark, sometimes rich. Internally, specific colors are used for identifiable purposes and the lighting is highly controlled. In Denver this is especially clear because of the geographic location. My first idea about the place was that it is about a certain kind of nakedness, an unusually harsh light, because you are a mile higher than normal. Inside the museum, the manipulation of the light and the tonality of the spaces becomes a replay of light effects in the city. In projects where pure color is used, I am responding to the light condition in the vicinity of the site and working within an emotional spectrum. The Stephen Lawrence Centre is explicitly about the choreography of light through color – about light and color as an emotive scenography. The centre is both a functional building and a monument, a combination that leads me to develop scenarios that play with this dialectic. You are never completely in one condition or the other; you oscillate between the two. The building is always reminding you of something else and enriching your experience.

_There are two key spaces in the Stephen Lawrence Centre: the entrance and, on the other side of the main building, a roof-level reception space and covered terrace with distant and local views. The red atrium is a gathering space, where the light filters through windows designed by the painter Chris Ofili, the passage linking the two buildings is lime green in color, and the ceiling of the reception space and terrace are bright yellow. This spatial sequence is largely independent of the functional program of the building and is realized in color and light. The interiors of the two Idea Stores were also based on the orchestration of light and ambience, especially the Whitechapel Road building, where the spaces are quite dim in some places and lighter in others. The darker spaces are more contained and the lighter spaces are more outward looking. The colored light washing the timber fins, which stiffen the external wall, unifies the spaces on each floor of the building.

_In developing the role of light in my architecture, I have been able to draw on experiences that I have had at different times in my life. After being brought up in Africa, I was very surprised by the light when my brothers and I first arrived in England. It was a new phenomenon, a completely different emotional experience – like being on another planet. The luminosity was much lower than we were used to, and I noticed how spaces opened up to take full advantage of it. My next experience of light was the time that I spent in Japan when I was a student. In Kyoto I made a set of drawings of a teahouse but what I was really studying was the light. When I measured that teahouse, it was not about materials. Although teahouses are described in terms of their material-artifact quality, the power of their architecture is in the way that light, materials, and geometry come together in an indivisible whole. This is very explicit in the raked sand of the dry seascape at the Ryoanji Zen Temple, a landscape that takes a phenomenon that is part of the larger visual culture of Japan and gives it a very singular presentation.

_One thing that I had not anticipated about Japan was that it would reawaken my memories of Africa and the light there. Africa has an exceptional luminosity and this has an all-pervasive effect on its architecture and the experience of space. But the consequences of the light vary greatly from one place to another and this is something that I recorded in my photographs of Africa's capital cities.

An earlier version of this essay was published in *David Adjaye Output,* ed. Peter Allison (Toto, 2011).

Facade detail, Sugar Hill, New York, 2011–2014   >

SUGAR HILL, NEW YORK, 2011–2014

Standing at the junction of 155th Street and St. Nicholas Avenue in Upper Harlem, the Sugar Hill building includes affordable housing for families and individuals on the upper floors, an early childhood center for over one hundred children at street level, and the Sugar Hill Children's Museum of Art and Storytelling at the lower ground level. The children's facilities are accommodated in a podium that covers the full extent of the site, the early childhood center features floor to ceiling glass and is organized around a series of courtyards, and the museum receives natural light from strategically placed roof lights. A rose pattern embossed in the precast concrete cladding panels recalls the area's bucolic past.

‹ Entrance plaza with view down 155th Street (left)

‹‹ Street view, St. Nicholas Avenue, showing row houses with sawtooth facade

Model view from lower end of site

Location plan

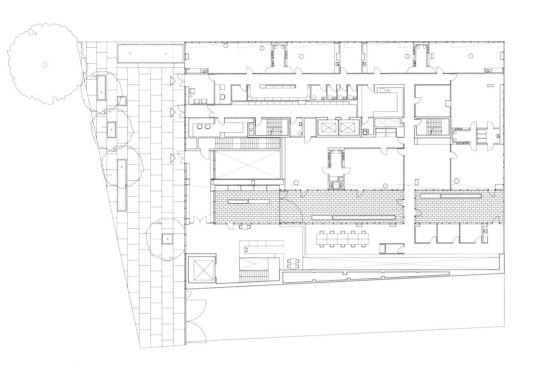

Plan, ground floor

‹ Early childhood center, courtyard

Early childhood center, teaching space

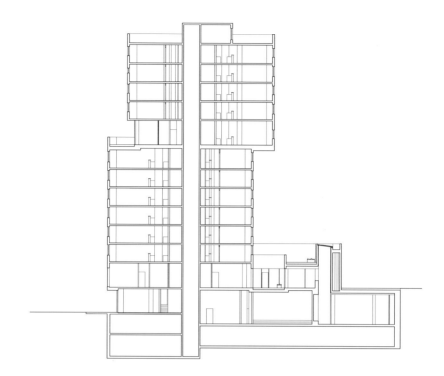

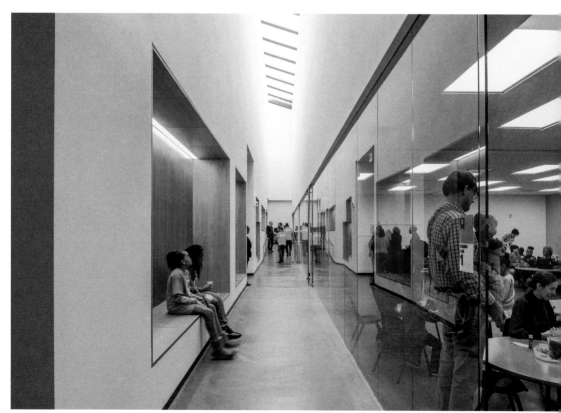

Section

Children's Museum of Art and Storytelling, roof-lit passage   Double-height gallery space   >

Ground floor residential entrance

Plan of typical apartment floor

Apartment interiors

>

Construction photos

TOWARD
BLACK

_HOUSES

Black and exteriority were part of my first building, which was the Elektra House. The site is at one end of a modest but well-proportioned terrace, but I was reluctant to mimic the neighboring houses. Our first scheme was very much to do with the context; it used the ground floor walls of an existing building as a base for a new extension. But as the design developed, it became increasingly clear that I wanted to shield the site from the public gaze, and the idea of making the architecture almost invisible became fascinating to me. It was clear that the iconography that would normally signify windows and doors had to be removed, and that anything that might suggest a particular formal reading had to be reduced. The design of Elektra is almost exclusively about the surprise of entering a light-filled interior world, and because there is very little space on the site for an architectural procession or threshold, the building itself sets up this contrast at an urban scale. For me, the best time to see the Elektra House is at dusk when, with its facade of dark-brown resin-coated plywood, it practically disappears. This was when I started thinking about building forms as voids. The facade of Elektra allows the terrace to have its own power, and the idea of the void seems to implicate the surroundings in a much more charged scenography.

_In Dirty House, which is not far from Elektra, the light-absorbing finish on the facade is a device for dealing with the building's many histories. We built the new house inside the walls of an old furniture factory and we had to carry out extensive repairs to the old walls, as well as increasing their height and thermal performance. If you look closely, you can still see these different finishes, but I decided to use a light-absorbing color, a deep brown-purple, as a way of moving the eye away from the visual titillation of seeing these textures in a picturesque way. Instead, the surface becomes a curious tapestry, a textured skin, which transforms the patched-up structure into a newly assembled whole. The struggle was how to create a sense of historical layers. Having seen the work of architects such as Hans Döllgast and Carlo Scarpa, who reveal layers of history in their work, I wanted to show the difference between what was existing and what was new. I was also looking for a way to present a new composition, which would be complete and no longer in a state of transition, and the light-absorbing finish – an anti-graffiti coating – fulfilled both these requirements. At the urban scale, our light-absorbing form reversed the conventional role of light on this street corner.

_While the Elektra House had developed on a largely intuitive basis, the evolution of the Dirty House was based on a series of very precise color studies. It was a time when we could use the computer to simulate materiality and to investigate what the end presence of the building was going to be. The studies showed that if we left the building in its original materials, it would lose the power that I knew it possessed. When we started to layer its appearance, using various filters, we realized that if we toned it down, the detailed materiality of the building had a less emphatic presence. We could then focus on more significant constructional statements, such as using the window to read the thickness of the wall. In this way, we were able to contextualize the position of the walls between the pavement at ground level and the cantilevered roof above. Due to the dark coating, you have simultaneous readings of this upright, monumental tube – as I see it – and this massively weighty masonry building.

_Light absorption is also relevant inside buildings. When I am dealing with smaller spaces, or trying to dematerialize the scale of an interior, certain kinds of darkness are helpful because they have an inherent sense of mystery. If it is difficult to read the edges of a space, it is possible to move many more things into the foreground than you would consider doing in a light-filled space. The curious thing about dark spaces is that they have this incredible effect of slowing down the heart rate, and they slow you down because the pupils of your eyes need time to see what you are doing. This effect of slowing down is a powerful design device, one that I was interested in exploring within the notion of interiority, and the Lost House is the test of this idea of dark space and dark-space choreography. The site for the house was previously a service yard and delivery zone for the building whose walls surround it on all sides;

there are no external views and it is all about interiority. This was not a situation in which there was strong south light available, so the preciousness of light had to be celebrated. The project sets up three vitrines, small internal courts, and the light from them is conditioned by what they contain: a pool, a stony landscape, and planting. Each of them has a different atmosphere and the light from them is very precious, not just as something you can bathe in or look through. In these special conditions, the conventional relationship between the larger enclosure and the vitrines is reversed, and the interiority becomes an exteriority. From a cave to a view: this condition sets up a very curious psychological state because you know that you are inside, but you have this sense of space unfolding in layers, as it would in a landscape. This is the effect of focusing on the low levels of light available, and of looking from darkness into light.

_In my approach to the design of houses, black is used as a design strategy, as a way to be very precise about my intentions, and to maintain the architectural focus. I am interested in certain kinds of forms and their ability to resonate in a way that moves them out of the iconography of memory into a different place. Darkness is a way of stopping you thinking that you know what you think you know; it is a device that is meant to make you more careful.

_PUBLIC BUILDINGS

The Bernie Grant Arts Centre was a fascinating exercise because it was the first time we could work across an assemblage of different scales and different programs. It is a major addition to an existing group of Edwardian civic buildings, which stand in line and face a landscaped space. Situated behind the retained frontage of one of the older buildings, the length and relative narrowness of the site were the main challenge, and our approach was to establish a tonal sequence – based on porosity or opaqueness – that would lead you from one end of the site to the other. Our graphic analysis told us where we could and could not use the types of material that we had in mind. If the picture plane was the line of the Edwardian facades facing the landscaped space, the intention was to use darker shades toward the front of the site, and slightly lighter ones to the rear. The new facades of the front building, the Hub, with its ticket office and teaching spaces, are clad in black ceramic tiles. The sidewalls of the Auditorium building are a dark-brown corrugated sheet, and the cladding panels of the Enterprise Building – at the back of the site and housing small offices for startups – are a brown cement-fiber board.

_The different cladding systems help to define the role of each building within the family group. On the Hub, the verticality of the tile cladding emphasizes the classical proportions of the building, without competing with the architecture of the re-tained facade. On the Auditorium building, the idea of a frozen reverberation, as a visual signifier, is presented by the zigzag pattern of the corrugated sheets of the sidewalls. Set at alternating diagonal angles, they produce a moiré pattern that works both horizontally and vertically, and creates a sense of movement down the length of the site. The Enterprise Building at the back of the site is more muted but the horizontal rhythm of its panels is syncopated with its immediate surroundings. Within this extended composition, the colors of the Purpleheart timber, which lines the foyer of the Auditorium, and the tiles on the Hub are a complementary pair, and the Purpleheart is a mediating color – a brown-purple – between the black tiles and the dark-brown sidewalls of the Auditorium. The Bernie Grant Arts Centre is a study of how dark absorption works in relation to proximity.

_At Bernie Grant, each building stands on a black concrete base that anchors it in position on the site, but the buildings that contribute to our market complex in Wakefield relate to one another on a different basis. The site is a transitional zone between the bus station and the city, and we wanted to create an open composition that would link the current situation with future developments. Our idea was to make a threshold to the city, and the project is about making a gateway that is a place in its own right, a fictionalized bucolic place between the city and where you have come from. This is the role of the black-painted frame. A second scale of architecture, relating to two retail halls and a storage building, reinforces the idea that you have arrived in a place that has already been defined. When you look at the secondary buildings, their expression and coloring are very muted, and they are almost interchangeable; they are additions to the frame, which remains the driver. The Wakefield building is the first time that we move away from monumental form to make a monumental frame. We wanted to establish the frame as a place-making silhouette, as a silhouetting presence that holds its place in the city.

_We tend to see individual buildings in terms of how they relate to their neighbors. This was certainly the case with Rivington Place, and the Museum of Contemporary Art Denver (MCAD). Rivington Place is about how to make an institutional building in a narrow Georgian street, and how to make a monumental form that does not seem to be falling on you. The program of the building was very clear and required us to stack several boxes on top of one another, so there was very little opportunity to manipulate the form. I was interested in developing a facade system that would allow me to have as much variety as possible, and result in a textural pattern that would reinforce the profile of the building. The precast concrete cladding panels take their geometry from the window patterns of nearby buildings, and their dimensions expand and contract to match the requirements on each facade. As well as absorbing light, the black finish unifies the elements of the facade within a single system and distinguishes our building from its light-reflecting neighbors. To draw attention to the public role of the building, I decided to develop the roofline and took a lead from the industrial rooflights that are found in this part of London. But instead of facing north like traditional examples, our rooflights face south because I wanted to animate the interior with a more playful light. The rooflights provide an urban silhouette and terminate the expansion and contraction of the facades. When you are in the street, it is an imposing building that is in retreat. I attribute this to the light-absorbing qualities of the dark facades; it is both a strong form and a relaxed form. It was important to the arts organizations it houses – Iniva (Institute of International Visual Arts) and Autograph ABP,

Entrance passage, *The Upper Room*, installation with Chris Ofili, London, 2002

Fireplace and passage to study, Seven, New York, 2004–2010

Top-floor studio space, Rivington Place, London, 2003–2007

Ribbed cladding, Auditorium, Bernie Grant Arts Centre,
London, 2002–2007

Enterprise Building, Bernie Grant Arts Centre, London, 2002–2007

The Washington Monument and north facade, National Museum of
African American History and Culture, Washington, DC, 2009–2016

which supports the work of black photographers – that Rivington should have this dual quality.

_HOUSES AND PUBLIC BUILDINGS IN THE UNITED STATES

The MCAD is located in a mixed-use area with a mid-rise tower, apartment blocks, and townhouses. These typologies are very expressive, in terms of the articulation of materials as planar reflecting systems. I felt that their presence exhausted the possibilities in terms of using a particular material to represent the public identity of the museum. Thinking of Dirty House, the alternative strategy was to make a void on this corner site – except that in this case it would be a luminous void. The idea of recessing and reflecting at the same time came out of a reading of Denver, which is a mile above sea level and has this extraordinary luminosity. Having completed our research, we selected a dark-gray glass as the primary cladding material for the body of the building. By day, the glass absorbs light and, like a soft mirror, reflects the surroundings; by night, the facades glow with light from inside the museum. The top floor is clad in untreated timber that will weather to a soft gray. As you look at the building, the glass enclosure has three key window moments. Sitting on the concrete base, a large window in a central position addresses 15th Street and, on the end facade, a second window looks over the entrance portal. Directly above the entrance, an urban window acknowledges the importance of 15th Street and its relation to Constitution Plaza at the heart of the city. The architecture has been reduced to these windows – you see the building as only having these openings. This device gives a monumentality to the project that signifies its public role.

_The museum and LN House are neighbors and are intended to be seen as a pair. More introverted in appearance, the black Corten steel cladding of the house has an opaque luminosity, to distinguish it from the translucent luminosity of the museum. All three American houses, Pitch Black in Brooklyn, Seven in midtown Manhattan, and LN, use blackness as an external strategy to make forms that are recessive in their imagery. If you look at where they are located, they are about marking end conditions in the urban context. They are not concerned with articulating new conditions, but with making full stops. They are houses with easily read profiles, to acknowledge where they stand, but dark color gives them a softer, less powerful presence, which is deferential to their neighbors. Their color on the street is also connected with how I saw the interiors. Entering Pitch Black, you have a sharp contrast, as the section is organized to create the most suitable lighting conditions for two artists, with light entering through the rear wall or through zenithal openings in the roof. At LN, where we wanted to create a quiet residential interior, the darkness moves into the house and then becomes gradually lighter on the upper floors.

_In Seven, the materiality and color of the exterior also feature in the interior. Concrete structure plays an essential role in this house, from the construction of retaining walls in the basement to bracing the sidewalls of the adjacent buildings on the floors above. We wanted the visual appearance of the concrete to reflect the conditions on the site when it had been largely cleared of the carriage house that previously stood there, allowing a close examination of the fabric and foundations of the surrounding buildings in a dim but dramatic light. Due to the aggregate we used, and how the concrete was placed in position, the surface textures in our house are highly responsive to the light, which is in keeping with how we saw the character of the site. Moving through the house, the structure becomes a device for opening up voids and we used a black mineral finish to unify the surface as a series of continuous planes. Concrete is celebrated as a material at the scale of the house and, internally its texture is pushed back in order to enjoy the spaces it creates.

_After researching the context for the Sugar Hill project and looking at the requirements in the brief, we were drawn to the idea of making an essentially opaque, masonry building. Standing on the edge of the valley of the Harlem River, we realized that the form we were making was very powerful and that we needed to quieten it down. The building is visible on all four sides and our studies showed that using a darker tone would give it an equivalent visual weight to the nearby mansion blocks. We took this discussion to the local community who supported the dark option, which led us to clad the building in dark-gray precast concrete panels. We had noticed that the mansion blocks in the area are decorated with plant forms embedded in the masonry and, having decided to make the fabric a recessive color, we decided to reverse the normal way of making decoration. Earlier in its history, the Sugar Hill area was known for its rose gardens and we decided to reference this memory by embossing a rose pattern in the surface of the concrete panels. Dry surfaces read differently from wet ones, and the pattern is only completely legible when it rains, or when the sunlight is at an oblique angle. At other times the pattern merges with the surface of the panels, whose color varies slightly due to the manufacturing process. I enjoy these variations because they create more richness in the process. There are similar variations in the screen-printed polypropylene panels on the facade of Pitch Black.

_In Washington, DC, the color of the National Museum of African American History and Culture (NMAAHC) is currently very changeable: from light bronze to a deep brown, depending on the strength and direction of the light. For me, the museum was always going to be a dark building. It will become very dirty, and I hope it will take on the patina of a bronze sculpture, the patina of something like a Henry Moore sculpture or some ancient classical artifact. This was always the intention: to make a bronze building, a dark metal building that would stand in contrast to the white stone buildings of the National Mall. Having discussed it with the client, we felt that the power of the building should be based on using a single material to establish a radical – but respectful and noble – relationship with the context. Bronze was the material of choice because of its long association with monuments, and because we were involved in a discussion about whether our project should be a building or an artifact. We wanted to embrace both possibilities: to be able to create sculptural relationships with the monument that is the most important object on the National Mall, the Washington Monument, and, at the same time, set up relationships with other buildings in the vicinity. In terms of the museum's program, there is a beautiful historical relationship between bronze, African history, and black culture. Bronze is one of the few metals that really does have a historical narrative with the African continent.

_THE AÏSHTI FOUNDATION, BEIRUT

The form and color of the Aïshti Foundation building in Beirut is intended to signify a new urban typology in this context. In the NMAAHC, we explored the ability of a second – outer – skin to register the identity of a new type of form, rather than using the building's program as an expression of difference. In Aïshti, we were looking at a hybrid condition: a commercial and cultural institution coming together to define a waterfront space for the city, when the business and institution were both private. The geometry of Aïshti is primarily to do with establishing a relationship to the geographical setting, the coastal hills and the sweeping shoreline to the north of the city center.

_Our buildings in Washington and Beirut are like nonidentical twins, in the sense that they explore very similar issues and come to different but related conclusions. Both buildings have complex programs and employ unifying forms to address the urban condition, and the social and political context, in each place. They are monumental buildings in sensitive places, and they have a power that comes from the silhouette and the form, not from a pattern of windows and doorways. When I sense that a form has developed this kind of power, I am not interested in increasing its luminosity. My approach is to make the form more absorbent and more recessive, as a basis for setting up relationships with the context. Going against classic modernism, which was about the reflection of light, this is a general strategy in my work. I sometimes do a bright building, but they are very much the exception.

FRANCIS A. GREGORY LIBRARY, WASHINGTON, DC, 2008–2012

Surrounded on three sides by forest, the site faces Alabama Avenue, which runs through several neighborhoods in the south of the city. The louvered roof filters the light reaching the interior and cantilevers over the front facade, forming an expansive porch. With a diagonal grid based on the expanding and contracting geometry of a cycad cone, the external cladding consists of alternately glazed and mirrored panels. The solid sections of the inner face of the wall are finished in Douglas Fir plywood. Arranged over two floors, the interior is a continuous open space with purpose-designed enclosures for certain activities.

Model showing canopy and entrance

Location plan

‹ Facade detail

Street view

›

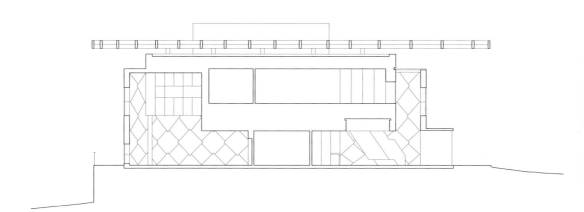

Plan, second-floor

Children's reading and program room (left), second floor

View of teen services space from second-floor conference space

>

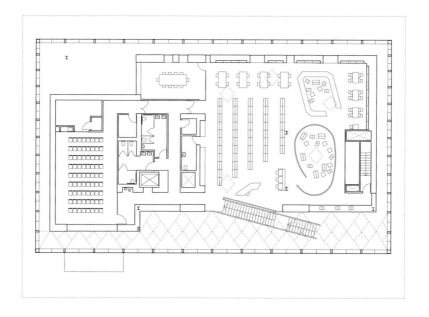

WILLIAM O. LOCKRIDGE LIBRARY, WASHINGTON, DC, 2008–2012

In the Bellevue neighborhood in the south of the city, the site has single-family houses on one side, and a cluster of mixed-use buildings on the other. The library is organized around an ascending route that follows the slope of the site and connects dedicated areas for children, teenagers, and adults. A series of detached pavilions provide activity spaces for different group of users, and two of the pavilions frame the main entrance. The dimensions of the long, glazed facade begin to match those of the mixed-use buildings, and the pavilions have a similar scale to the nearby houses.

Model showing position of staircase on long facade

< Pavilions framing an external gathering space

Location plan

Street view showing children's pavilion (left), teen pavilion (center), and adults' pavilion (right)

>

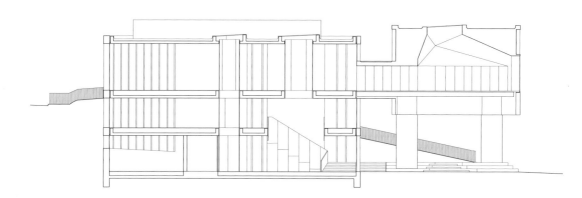

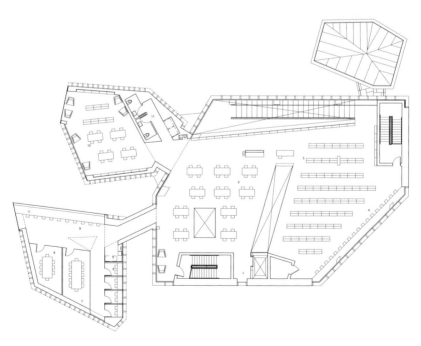

Long staircase, second floor

Plan, third floor

Adult reading room, third floor

Entrance to teen pavilion, third floor

Entrance to adult pavilion, third floor

›

»

CONSTRUCTED NARRATIVES

_THE DEMOCRACY OF KNOWLEDGE

In the planning stage of my exhibition at the Haus der Kunst in Munich in 2015, we used the phrase "the democracy of knowledge" to anchor the discussion relating to the design of our public buildings. We were thinking about how these buildings exist to provide information for citizens, and their role in representing institutions and authority. In cities they are places where certain groups in society – diverse groups that are not fully integrated – feel comfortable and can potentially engage with the wider community. My idea was to create structures that, from an institutional point of view, are independent in their iconography and encourage the widest possible access. A sense of utility in the provision of facilities is one strategy that I have explored. How do buildings become less institutional and more utilitarian in their availability to citizens? If they take on this quality, like other everyday products, it encourages a greater mobility of knowledge across society. "The democracy of knowledge" refers to the broad principles on which these projects were generated.

_My involvement with designing buildings of this type began with winning commissions for the Nobel Peace Center and the Idea Store buildings in the early years of the century. Engaging with the needs of communities often raised questions that were difficult to define and, in relation to the physical environment, were invisible. These questions opened up a wide range of issues that, in my experience, architecture had not begun to negotiate. I remember having discussions with the client for the Idea Stores about exceptionally poor literacy rates and the need to encourage access to the language courses in our buildings. At the same time, we were visiting schools in the area and found the experience of entering them quite forbidding. I was shocked. The infrastructure was in place and the software was available, but the hardware was a hindrance to established criteria concerning the need for a knowledge base in society. Open access ensures that people can operate on an equal basis and to the best of their ability. I became aware of this issue when, as a young student, I designed a disability center and discovered that such places had been largely ignored by designers

– they had been left to technicians. When I began to teach architecture, we always looked for new typologies, rather than ones that had been tried and tested, to understand how architecture can impact on every part of the environment. What happens if you work at that lowest level in society? What impact does it have in these communities? That became my primary focus. In our design for the Nobel Peace Center, the way in which we characterized the main spaces was intended to connect with people's fundamental experiences of war and peace, regardless of their origins or culture. In the Idea Store buildings, we continued the spatial arrangements of the nearby street markets into the building, to break down perceived boundaries and open up the interiors to the community.

_The fact that we aim to think through basic questions relating to the role of buildings does not mean that such thoughts are explicitly legible in the buildings themselves. I believe that the forces that are being understood, analyzed, or thought through imbue the project with a certain provenance, and whether they are in some way represented or legible is irrelevant. My experience is that the content of the program behind the building is something that people can relate to, regardless of the degree to which it is expressed in the architecture. I am not completely clear how this happens, but the wider relevance – the sense of engagement – is picked up by enough people for it to be significant. Making this connection is the basic move for me; it involves looking at situations from a new perspective and understanding how architecture might be relevant. When this happens, after the building has been occupied, you have a sense of recognition that goes beyond mimicry or simulation. Our design for the Museum of Contemporary Art Denver was about providing a type of gathering space that was missing from the city, by creating an environment with the spatial characteristics of Denver at a time when it was a more pedestrian-friendly city. This reading of the interior of the museum only comes to life when there are people looking at exhibitions or attending events there.

_ADDRESSING COMMUNITIES

Having a range of activities under the same roof can enhance the experience of using a building, but it is not essential; an institution with one main purpose can still connect with the community at many different levels. The advantage of multiple offerings is that they can be arranged like fruit on a tree, giving personal choice and a range of possible destinations, which was the situation at the Idea Store Whitechapel and the Bernie Grant Arts Centre. A range of activities establishes a kind of menu for the community, but the alternative – a singular offering that can be approached by different routes – has real potential. The critical consideration is to do with how the requirements in the design brief are translated into built fabric.

_When there are more than one or two destinations in a building, I become much more precise about the notion of the journey, which can be a useful organizational device. If you look at the Francis A. Gregory Library, for example, the basis for making a particular journey is only loosely presented, as most of the facilities are accessed in the main space. In the William O. Lockridge Library, the situation is very different as the floors are stacked up in response to the sloping site. The circulation route is more highly defined and takes people to a variety of destinations, which enjoy specific relationships with each other and with the surrounding neighborhood. This degree of complexity strengthens the narrative – established by the journey from the exterior to the interior and back again – and the architecture becomes more precise. The irony is that both libraries have the same program – it is the differences between the sites that lead to divergent design strategies. The verticality of the William O. Lockridge arrangement prevented me from displaying the content on a single occasion, and I had to create trajectories for people to encounter a range of services, without appearing to drag them around. This is an example where, in terms of experience, the main route establishes a narrative that draws you onward.

_My interest in displaying content is the reason why I photographed so many markets and street traders in my book on Africa's capital cities. Markets are a key communal act. Not

"communal" in the sense that we collectively make them together, but because they represent a shared moment in the idea of
cities throughout history. There is something about them that
is very primal and speaks about the public life of the citizen,
the notion of exchange and the collective – a dense condition of
merchandise and exchange. With voyeurism and all the social
nuances that play out there, they are a perfect cosmos of the
potential of life in the city with strangers. They are fascinating
spaces to observe. Whenever I travel anywhere, I search out
the market because of the way it helps me to sense the person-
ality of a place. The details of the displays and the ad hoc nature
of their organization always make connections with the physical context and the geographic location of the city. Apart from
their rootedness, they are complex programmatic entities and,
being open-ended, they can be very suggestive.

_PLACE AND RITUAL

Geographic location was a factor in the design of the Idea Store
buildings in London and in the two neighborhood libraries
we designed in Washington, DC. Each of the London buildings
is in a physically dense location and the external form is a
response to the scale and position of neighboring buildings,
and to the character of nearby thoroughfares. The libraries
in Washington, DC, on the other hand, are in an area of the
city where the forest landscape has more continuity than the
buildings. Designed as pavilions – freestanding in the case of
Francis A. Gregory and clustered at William O. Lockridge – the
libraries work with this condition. The experience of using
the Idea Stores and the Washington libraries is closely informed
by the relationship that each building has to its geographic
hinterland. I am continually searching for those forces in order
to create as much specificity as possible in the work.
_Adding to the sense of place is critical. Place making is about
reinforcing the sense of daily ritual, whether the place in question is about studying, buying fruit, recreation, or whatever.
The way that society develops patterns of association that
become part of the human psyche is a really powerful consideration in architecture and form making. As architects, we are

often too obsessed with the building, when the fundamental issue is adding to the place and to what the place represents. This is where we can succeed: when the building is adopted into the pattern and ritual of people's lives. It involves the ongoing experiences of a community and what happens when you introduce a new entity. When we showed ten public buildings in an exhibition at London's Whitechapel Gallery in 2006, each project was accompanied by a series of step-by-step drawings showing how the external envelope of the building had developed in response to immediate context. My aim was to reflect the immediate conditions in which we were working, and for the new building to extend or amplify the local sense of place.

_The analytical drawings in the Whitechapel exhibition reflected the conclusions we had reached later in the design process. Although I am self-conscious about what I am aiming for, it takes time to understand all the factors at play in any situation. The point at which the issues come into focus marks the end of an important stage in the development process. That is the subjective authoring moment, the moment of creation when the forces involved translate into a design proposal. I am at my sharpest when all the questions around a project have been fleshed out, all the issues that I am concerned about in terms of location, program, geography, typology, and place making. As the uncertainty begins to settle, I become more precise in terms of understanding how I can bring the different strands together. The creative moment is when we have been through all the preliminaries, and depends on how I am seeing the forces and how I believe the issues coming out of a situation can be resolved. Before that, when my understanding is less complete, I am more ambiguous about what the building is and how it works. The creative moment activates the arsenal of types that I have in my mind's eye. As I run through them, a series of tests come to mind, depending on where I have decided to focus. There are clarifying strategies and there are what I call hybridizing or deforming strategies. It all depends on what the place needs; sometimes it needs more complexity and at other times it needs clarity.

CONSTRUCTED NARRATIVES

View down staircase, Francis A. Gregory Library,
Washington, DC, 2008–2012

Covered gathering space, William O. Lockridge Library,
Washington, DC, 2008–2012

West facing atrium, National Museum of African
American History and Culture, Washington, DC, 2009–2016

Detail of west facade, Aïshti Foundation, Beirut, Lebanon,
2012–2015

Roof terrace, Stephen Lawrence Centre, London,
2004–2007

_For people to engage with the institutions we design, I look to establish a scenario that connects with their immediate experience. It might be the atmosphere in a place, the character of the landscape, or the nature of the urban condition – anything that has the potential for making relevant connections and triggering some kind of intrigue. Understanding a situation, in terms of what aspects are likely to have most potential for anchoring a project, involves a degree of informed intuition, but by making these connections, it is possible to amplify certain conditions and engage with environmental and locational issues. It is all about responding to the immediate experience of being somewhere and building on that, giving it depth or a focus it may not have had previously. In some cases, we have angled facades to accentuate a certain view or created an external gathering space, from which to appreciate the urban scene. The double-facade arrangement that I often use is a useful tool in manipulating the exterior and setting up relationships. The outer cloak simplifies the building's profile in the urban context, and the void between the inner and outer facade, which improves thermal and acoustic performance, is responsive to light conditions, adding a sense of intrigue.

_JOURNEYS

As an architect, it is difficult to avoid being in a position where you are expected to offer some sort of guidance. Our business is to give clues and to trigger certain automatic responses in the mind about how you approach a given situation. We work within certain conventions and build a narrative by making relationships with nature and the urban context, to suggest a sympathetic way of approaching things. The successful strategies are the ones that allow for a more natural sense of awareness and avoid making dictatorial impositions. Depending on the situation, you have to create the right sense of distance and space, to allow the mind to absorb and conceptualize enough information before moving on. People need time and space to be able to read things in their own way.

_With this in mind, I need to be clear about where people begin and end their journeys, and about whether these places need to be articulated or can remain neutral in their expression. Movement spaces can be neutral or highly specific in character, as they take you from one place to another. Lacking the focus of a destination, they can be powerful encounter spaces, powerful orientation spaces, or spaces for reading and understanding the relevant issues. In the Idea Store Whitechapel and the National Museum of African American History and Culture (NMAAHC), for example, there are promenade spaces that are essential to the overall function of the building and at the same time allow people to reflect on what is on offer and where they are in the city. In the Disc element of the Moscow School of Management Skolkovo, the movement spaces that connect the various teaching departments have a similar double role. Our thinking was that the students would learn from each other, as well as their teachers, and the free areas in the Disc are for that kind of interchange.

_Part of my method is to play the formal and the informal against each other. I sometimes manipulate the conventions that apply to movement and destination spaces as part of a strategy for setting up a new level ground that avoids privileging or discriminating against anyone who may arrive there. By working between the traditional polarities, it is possible to set up a neutral plane where people can be more open, in terms of what they engage with and how they understand it. This was the concept behind making the various levels in the foyer to the Bernie Grant Auditorium, to give people an opportunity to find a personal location, as they move in or out of the auditorium. There may be several places in a project with this kind of freedom and the challenge for me is to maintain a unity of purpose – an overall sense of identity – that is sufficiently strong to allow for a degree of looseness between the parts. The identity of an institution is the basis on which it makes external connections, while a looseness between the parts allows for the multiple shifts that are necessary for progress.

_I am always drawing the limits of where people can go – I am always asking myself that question. The ultimate freedom is the completely unauthored network, which exists on the web. It is a matrix that can allow for any possibility or narrative.

But the arrangements in buildings require so much collective knowledge that we are a long way from reaching the point where we can make architecture on a purely systematic basis. The risk of that kind of system is that it plays to those who are in the know and short-circuits others. For me, a public project is still about allowing the greatest number of people to experience the maximum benefit from every part of the building. In the NMAAHC, there is no ambiguity about how the circulation works. From the monumental entrance hall, the main options are to go down to the History Galleries or up to the Corona, where there are further exhibits and views of the National Mall and the city. The choices are clear and presented without any suggestion of a hierarchy. In the History Galleries, people will be encouraged to follow a certain route when the building opens, to give them the best chance of taking in a wide range of exhibits that have never been presented in one place before. When the material is better known, it may be more interesting for people to wander freely, and it will be fascinating when we reach that stage.

_THE BODY

If the interior is about movement and opportunity, the exterior concerns what I call "the body" in architecture. It is about achieving a resolution in the assemblage – a coherent arrangement of the constituent parts of the brief – and then creating a certain dress, a way of being in the world. I only understand what that should be after I have organized the entire project. At that point, I have what I need and can understand this final step. I am still not happy with the late modernist, high-tech idea of simply expressing the parts, as a kind of biology. I am fascinated with how new concepts present themselves in the contemporary city, what information is being given out about these concepts and the ways people access them. Many of my buildings have an inner skin and an outer facade, and with this arrangement I can organize the facade with both the interior of the building and the scale of the city in mind. I have a degree of freedom to manipulate the relationship between the building's interiors and the city, to suggest something about the role

of the building at a scale that is legible in the wider city and beyond. I normally stop the outer facade above ground level, and at this point the architecture is about moving in and out of the building. The NMAAHC is an example of this arrangement.
_In detail, the outer facades of my buildings are constructed of panels whose edges make a geometric lattice that envelops the exterior. As the outer skin is often detached from the main structure, I can manipulate the pattern of the lattice in relation to the proportions of the building, the dimensions of the site, and the scale of neighboring buildings and spaces. Using these abstract patterns, I am trying to do two things that appear to be contradictory. The patterns are intended to reveal the form and scale of each building as clearly as possible and, at the same time, to suggest that this form is not completely real. The patterns fail to explain many aspects of the building. As abstractions, they leave a great deal to the imagination, in terms of understanding the integrity of the structure or the internal organization of the building. This gap in how the building is perceived is fascinating. It creates an opportunity for the viewer to complete the picture in their own way, depending on what they see as most relevant – atmosphere, luminosity, or something more specific. This openness is a powerful tool as it allows for an understanding that goes beyond immediate circumstances. The more you close down the definition of the form – like a tomb – the more specific is its identity. Conversely, opening up the reading of the form allows it to lead many lives. This is not about transparency: it is about breaking down matter so that it is no longer a sealed entity.

NATIONAL MUSEUM OF AFRICAN AMERICAN HISTORY AND CULTURE, WASHINGTON, DC, 2009–2016

The museum occupied the last remaining site on the National Mall, on a corner where the Capitol Hill axis meets the White House axis, and is the closest of the Smithsonian museums to the Washington Monument. Positioned in relation to existing buildings, the footprint of the Corona is smaller than that of the History Galleries, which are sixty feet below street level. The bronze finish, latticework facades provide thermal protection for the inner volume of the Corona, and the circulation route to the upper levels offers views of the surrounding monuments. On the Capitol Hill axis, the South Porch frames the entrance to Heritage Hall.

Model showing South Porch

Location plan

‹ East facade, looking south on 14th Street

Night view of the National Mall with the museum (left) and the United States Capitol (right) ›

A Washington Monument
B Old Post Office, Federal Triangle
C The Capitol
D Mall Panoramic
E The White House
F Jefferson Memorial
G Lincoln Memorial
H Martin Luther King Memorial
I East Building, National Gallery of Art
J Hirshhorn Museum
K The Castle

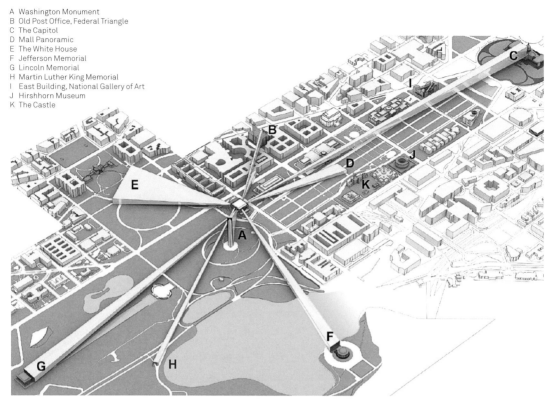

< Schematic drawing showing the monuments visible from the museum

South Porch and facade

Historic ironwork in New Orleans (left) and Charleston (right)

View showing the White House, the Washington Monument, and the Potomac River, with the museum on the left

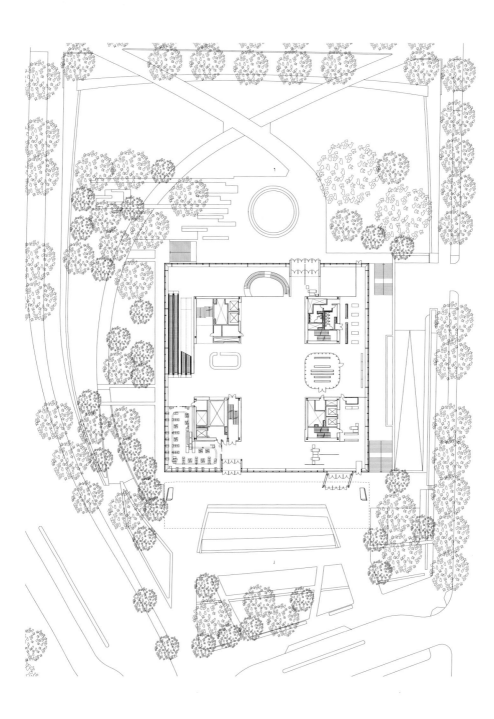

Ground-floor plan showing Heritage Hall (center),
Monumental Stair (curved), and Oculus (above)

Heritage Hall

Entrance bridge and lower section of the Monumental Stair

〉

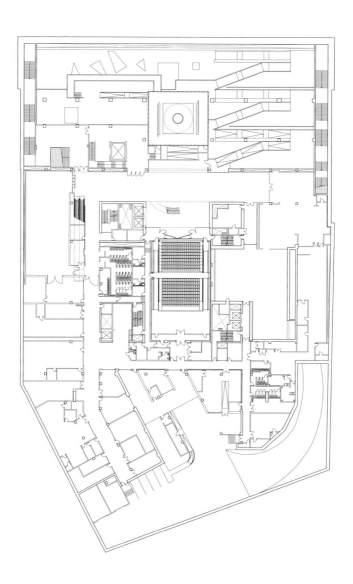

Concourse-level plan showing Auditorium (center),
History Galleries, and Contemplative Court (above)

Monumental Stair, Concourse Level

History Galleries, below Concourse Level

>

>>

≪ West facing atrium

< Interior view of facade system

Plan, second floor

North facing atrium, second floor

Interior view of the bronze finish cladding and
the Washington Monument

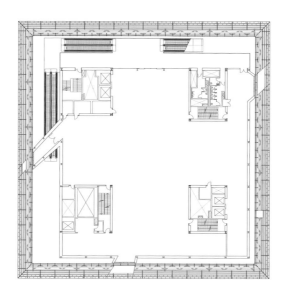

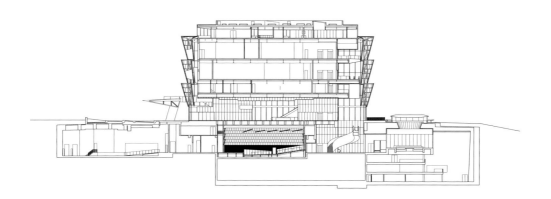

Construction photos

View across the Potomac River with Lincoln Memorial (left), museum and Washington Monument (center), and the dome of United States Capitol (right)   >>

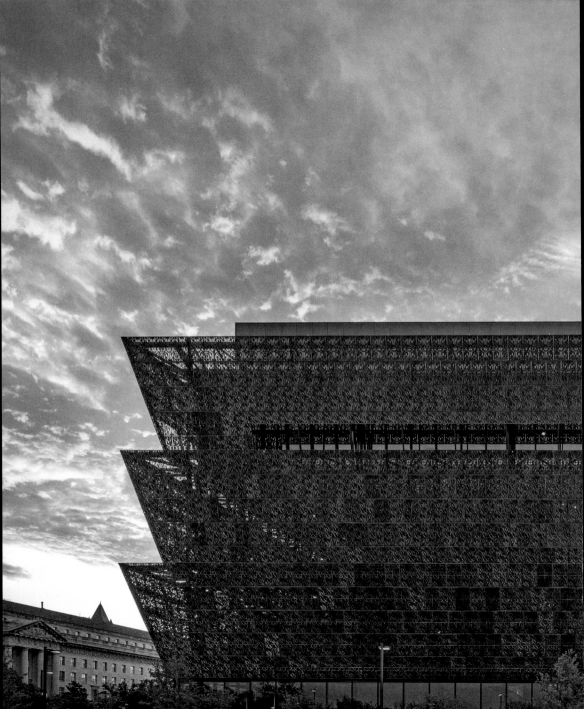

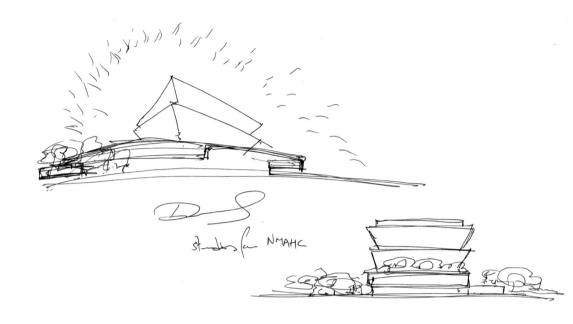

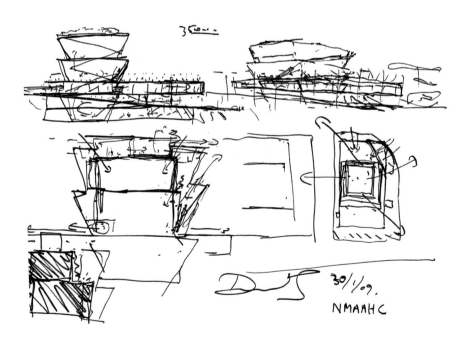

‹ West facade, evening

Study of plinth and Corona

Study showing the ascending route (top left)

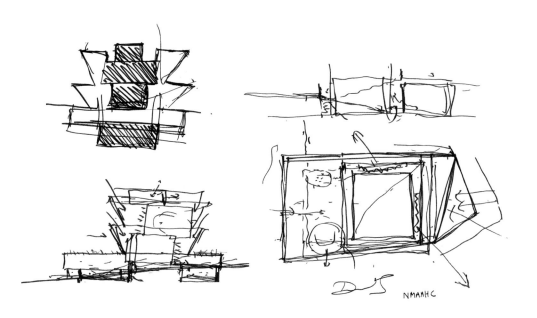

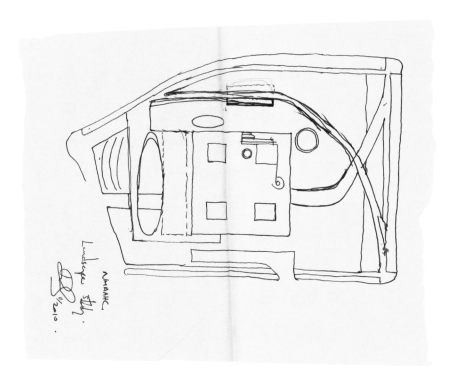

Study showing suspended volumes (top left)

Site layout

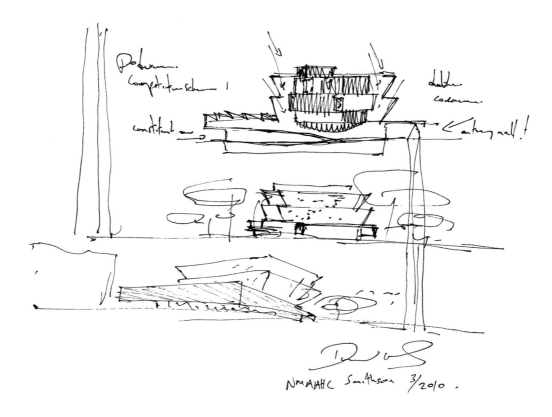

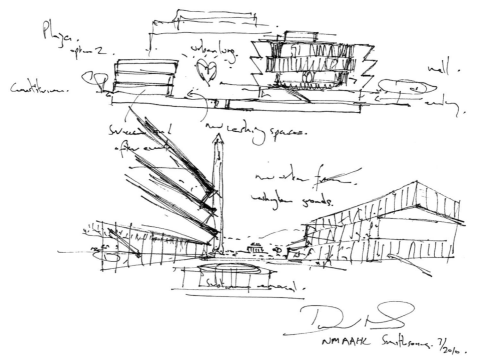

Study showing relationship between the museum and the Washington Monument

The "urban lung" on Constitution Avenue

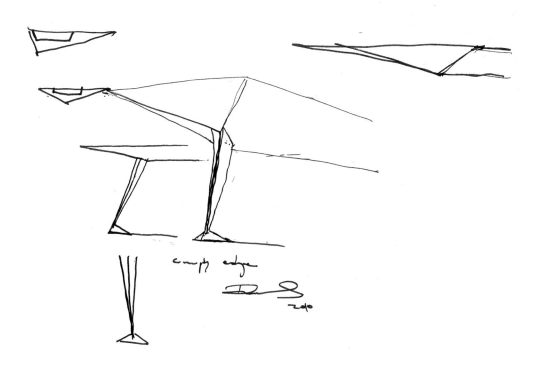

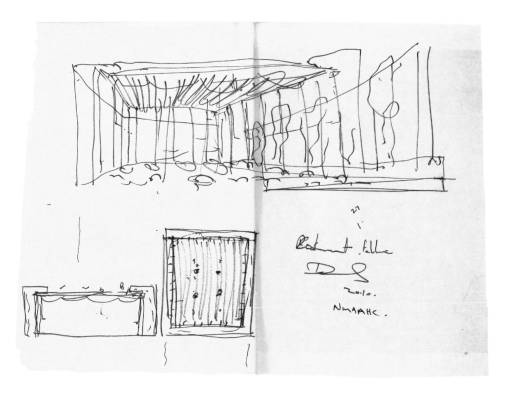

The South Porch

The restaurant space

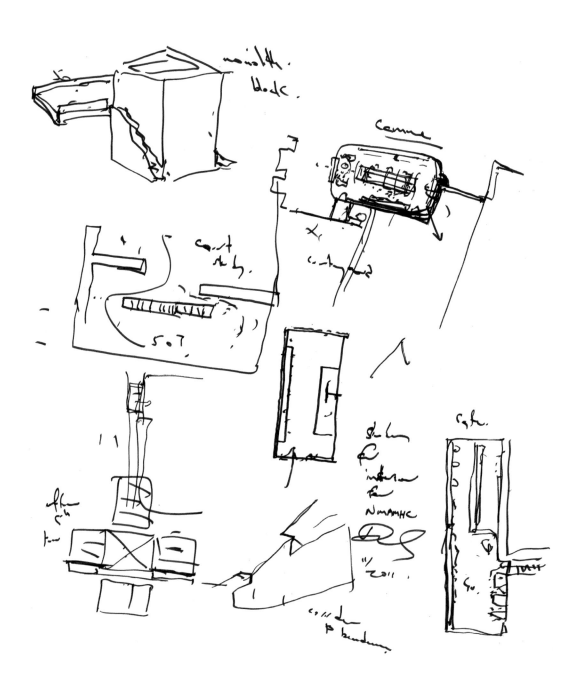

Special spaces

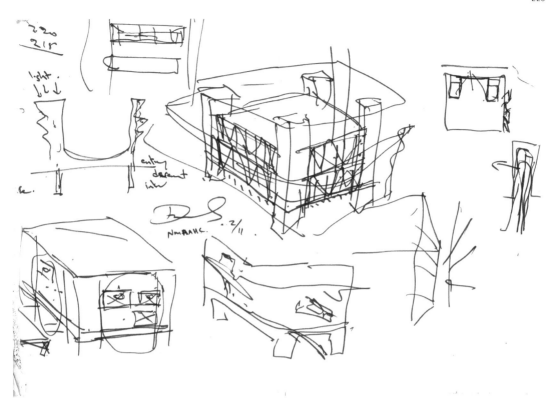

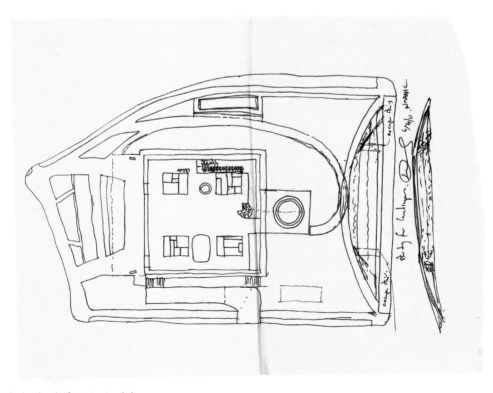

Study showing the four structural piers

Plan showing the position of the four piers

ACTIVATING THE SECTION

_BUILDING TYPES

In the design phase, I often run through a list of building types that have some connection with what we are doing. The criteria for the list are always quite loose, so I could be looking at everything from the monument to the public market, through to the shrine, the church, the cathedral, the palace, and the house. I am also thinking about how each of these has evolved – the medieval house, the renaissance house, and the twentieth-century house – and about the different construction techniques employed and what they represent. In doing this, I am checking if there are any connections and possible links with the project in hand. I am interested in how a situation in the present might connect with the way in which comparable buildings have been handled previously, and in establishing an architectural genealogy, in terms of relevant buildings or building systems, rather than authors. This is when I start to see the new project in terms of its relation to precedent, and how it might move forward based on translation or hybridization.

_Thinking about building types can raise issues that extend beyond the physical context of the project. The role of types in a particular context is an important consideration but I am also interested in the precision and the broader history of the subject. Although the projects are fixed in time and space, there is this body of knowledge called "Architecture," which is universal to the human experience, and this is why my interest in types is independent of the function of the project I am working on, and why I do not always see types as complete entities. I may be looking at volume, geometry or section – I very rarely look at the complete building. With the program of my building as the starting point, understanding the immediate situation in relation to a broader architectural view clarifies what I need to focus on and which considerations I can put aside. It defines the area I shall be working in and, having done that, opens up a range of possibilities.

_There are elements in my buildings that reappear in different forms, depending on the project and where it is. I am interested in how systems work in a variety of conditions, so there is a larger enquiry and a degree of testing that connects many of the projects. I am not looking for a universal solution that is applicable in all circumstances, but I need to understand the range of conditions in which a particular form of construction or building section is applicable. To extend the range, it is necessary to make adjustments or radical revisions to the system I started with, and this process can lead to architectural solutions that are closely tailored to their locations. If you look at how I organize the sections of buildings, there is probably an arsenal of half a dozen sections that I keep returning to. I am fascinated by those sections as archetypes and constantly test their possibilities. My work is a collection of organizational devices that are loosely connected within a larger network of possibilities, but they need to be grounded on each occasion that I use them.

_I often work with volumes that express the maximum dimensions of the site. I love the idea that a human being – a person – exists in the constructed narrative of the world and that architecture can talk about this condition. Being able to take in basic dimensions is important to our understanding, but too often architecture gets in the way, playing to received ideas about how the city should look. I am interested in expressing the shifts and iterations that result from adapting a larger organization to the as-found conditions on a site, whether they involve differences in level, discontinuities in the boundary condition, or degrees of openness to the surrounding view. I take an analytical approach to existing conditions, but placing the overall dimension in view is the primary move. Having this priority often leads to me using rectangular forms that have been distorted, gentle parallelograms whose angles connect with conditions in the wider context.

_SQUARE PLANS

My ideal public building has a square plan and is visible from all sides. The inherent symmetry of this form recommends it for public buildings, as it avoids the formal uncertainties that can attach themselves to other volumes. It has the same basic identity when seen from any direction. This lack of ambiguity has sometimes been used as a basis for generating complexity, but I am drawn to in these cubic forms for their intrinsic transparency. I am not talking about literal transparency but about the possibility of taking in and understanding the overall dimensions of the project. The form reveals its depth and indicates the distance from the edge of the plan to the center. Knowing that people are aware of this distance is a significant consideration in how I organize these buildings. The experience of moving toward the center of the plan is reversed as you move outward back to the edge, but the basic measurement is identical and that knowledge helps people to navigate the interior. This type of organization still has a part to play when the site conditions are not completely symmetrical, which was the case at the Idea Store Whitechapel and the Museum of Contemporary Art Denver, as well as on the freestanding sites for the Francis A. Gregory Library and the National Museum of African American History and Culture (NMAAHC).

_The spaces I locate at the heart of the plan, and on the perimeter, acknowledge their different locations. I experimented with this arrangement in the Elektra House, where the centrally placed living space is protected on both sides by narrow, double-height spaces that connect with the exterior. On the ground floor of the NMAAHC, Heritage Hall enjoys a similar relationship to the building's periphery. Examples of square-shaped public buildings in history are not as common as you would expect, as the majority are rectangles. The anti-chamber at Luxor has this type of cubic volume and the Great Mosque of Cordoba is an important model – it is almost, but not quite square. There are several square-plan buildings in Le Corbusier's work, from the Villa Savoye to the Assembly Building in Chandigarh, and the square was important to Louis Khan, in designing the Jewish Community Center near Trenton, for example. They are usually deployed to make a public place, to unify and bring people together. If you look at mandala drawings or studies of Persian gardens, the combinations of squares and circles are really compelling. They suggest an amazing moment, an ideal creation.

_URBAN TUBES

A second group of buildings in my work employs linear plans and tubular volumes. In terms of their exterior and interior impact, tubular volumes are places that make us aware of the physical body, whether we happen to be in a landscape or the interior of a building. They are a common experience in the city – as an alley, lane, mews, or path – but are more difficult to find as an internal condition. To make an interior version of the external condition is a fascinating exploration because there is a special kind of power in bringing external dimensions to the interior of a building. There is something restful about introducing the continuous perspective associated with these external spaces to the interior world; it breaks with the usual pattern of making rooms as specific entities, and leads to the possibility of the interior as an unfolding sequence. It is about bringing the architecture of external spaces to the interior of buildings, bringing the inclusive architecture of the city into the building.

_If the cubic buildings I discussed earlier present a clear image to the outside world, the linear buildings are ambiguous in their composition and their arrangement – their ambiguity is their pleasure. When I am focused on these tube-like forms, I am primarily interested in the interior as a space of encounter. This is my starting point for any design, because these buildings are about engaging with the interior as a separate entity from the exterior. I rarely enter a tube from the end, but use the location of the ends as anchor points for the journey between them. I am fascinated by the prospect of making a casual entrance at some point on the side and suddenly seeing the long dimensions sweeping away in either direction. Then you would naturally want to check out the end points, which are always very specific and never the same. Where you enter establishes the sequence and the doorway can be anywhere, depending on what the program demands. The ends of the Idea Store Chrisp Street address a public square and nearby houses. In the Auditorium building at the Bernie Grant Arts Centre and at the Aïshti Foundation, the accommodation is organized on a linear basis, but without having a single continuous space from one end to the other. Compared with the cubic form, which accounts for many of my institutional buildings, these bar-like buildings are about making connections between places in the city.

_The nineteenth-century galleria is an abstract and very powerful version of this idea of architecture as an extended system; these enclosed streets tapped into, and somehow summarized, the urban contexts where they stood. My fascination with tubular forms comes from looking at the sculpture of Donald Judd, who uses continuous loops as part of a very effective communication system. At his foundation at Martha in Texas he made these sculptures that consist of a series of tubular sections going into the desert, framing the landscape in collective or disjointed ways. It may seem tenuous but I connect this experience with the tubular living spaces in Marcel Breuer's houses, that moment in modernism when experiencing the interior depended on having a relationship with an external condition. There are similar set-ups in the work of Amancio Williams in Argentina and Lina Bo Bardi in Brazil.

_TRIANGLES

In certain conditions I am drawn to triangular forms. If cubic forms are highly legible and suggest accessibility, the triangle is the moment of form guiding – it is a guiding device. When you shift into an angle, you move from the neutrality of an orthogonal system to directionality and a specific form of control. That moment is all about understanding the manipulative power of architecture. For me, it represents the strongest moment of authoring: "I insist you do this." The triangle is fascinating because it is so controlling in terms of its impact on the plan. When I need to focus on something or set up a special emphasis, the triangle is the form that seems to succeed in dealing with the complexity of the problem. But it is inherently unstable and usually needs a counterpoint, a fixed point in the context or in the project itself, which acts as an anchor. In the Stephen Lawrence Centre, the anchor is the smaller building that stands on a single, sturdy column; it pins the whole project to the site and stops the larger building from flying off.

Tubular interior, Idea Store Chrisp Street, London, 2002–2004

The anchor building (left), Stephen Lawrence Centre, London, 2004–2007

Zenithal light in central space, Museum of Contemporary Art Denver, Denver, 2004–2007 >

View across light shaft, William O. Lockridge Library, Washington, DC, 2008–2012

A cluster of volumes on a table, Idea Store Whitechapel, London, 2001–2005

_The triangle presents an enigmatic form that is especially rele-
vant to the notion of the memorial, because the combination
of incompleteness and directionality acts as an emotive trigger
to further enquiry. But it is not a form that I would only link
with race, which was the case in the Stephen Lawrence Centre.
I associate it more generally with memory and commemora-
tion, or issues that need to be approached from a specific direction. I have explored the complexity of the triangle as a gener-
ative form, and how to stabilize it, in several pavilion projects.
Horizon sets up a tension between the directionality of the
main space, looking toward the view, and the entrance enclosure, which acts as the anchor. In Genesis, it is the shaft of light
from the oculus in the roof that pins the structure to the site.

_CLUSTERS

Whenever possible, I employ a version of one of the forms
I have discussed, but there are times when, due to the complexity of the context or the demands of the program, I need to
employ several of them at once. The cluster type is an effective
response to what I call "no-grid" conditions, areas where there
are discontinuities in plan and section. In this type of condition I can adjust different parts of my cluster to connect with
the surrounding conditions, and the larger project develops a
degree of complexity without becoming over-complicated. Pursuing this type of strategy at the Bernie Grant Arts Centre gave
us the opportunity to set up a new public square that connects
existing and new buildings, and extends the landscape of nearby Tottenham Green onto our site. The three buildings that
make up the center have different functions, but they have a
family likeness that gives them a larger presence in the community. The Hub is cubic and the Auditorium and Enterprise
buildings are tubular, and their individual scale, configuration,
and materiality reflect their positions on the site.

_The notion of the cluster also figures in the design of single
buildings. At Rivington Place, for example, our building forms
a cluster with its neighbors, including a parallel building
with a repetitive window pattern, and Shoreditch Town Hall.
The scale and fenestration of our building is intended to make

connections with the surrounding fabric, helping to define a larger environment with a specific sense of place. In Washington, DC, the site for the NMAAHC presented a similar situation but in reverse. The National Mall, with the United States Capitol on the main axis and the White House on a cross-axis, represents one of the most coherently planned groups of buildings in the world and the design problem was less to do with acknowledging this monumental backdrop and more to do with adding a new voice – a sufficiently distinctive voice to encourage a re-reading of the overview presented by the existing composition. Our proposal is intended to complement its neighbors in scale and composition and to suggest, through its materiality and detailing, an alternative lineage for the architecture of some of our neighbors.

_In other projects, because of the site or the brief, we have layered several functions together, so that they retain their separate identities and can be read as compressed or consolidated clusters. The Idea Store Whitechapel, the Moscow School of Management Skolkovo, and Sugar Hill are organized around a raised datum level, a structural table with distinctive volumes rising above. I see the city as a process of sedimentation in which different use patterns and systems of construction contribute successive layers of development. The coexistence of these layers contributes to the diversity of the contemporary urban environment, and our urban projects are about exploring this time-based view of the city. The concept of a "slice of time" is something I am very interested in. It can be about a time to come – a time of increased collaboration – that involves setting up a datum and then talking about a cluster that moves forward, beyond that line. Thinking about time raises questions on our current prospects, as we review the future; architecture can increase connectivity and help us to understand the circumstances of contemporary life.

_TABLES

The table is a further type that I am exploring, as a structural form and as a visual device. Its primary purpose, in my mind, is to do with reducing or lowering the atmosphere. In the NMAAHC, this involves a hybrid condition because the structure facing the Mall, the entrance canopy, is an enclosing frame and the inner volume is a cube. These are the components that I am bringing together – it is a moment of extreme hybridity that I am testing. The idea is to use the table, the entrance canopy in this case, to literally lower the sky. It may sound simplistic but the intention is to focus the atmosphere at a lower level, giving people a greater awareness of where they are on a wider plane. This focus on the horizontal is about creating conviviality and a sense of intimacy. Wakefield Market Hall is the concise example and the Skolkovo building, where the Disc appears to support the buildings above, is the complex version. At Sugar Hill and in the Washington museum the table is an organizational device, a raised datum that connects the main elements of each building and relates them to the context. In the NMAAHC, the table is more of a conceptual imposition on other moves that I am making.

_LIGHT AS A REGISTER OF PLACE

Drawing a cross section is an opportunity to study the building as a complete system. It shows how different floors are related, how the ground plane and the roof are connected, whether the roof is accessible. A large part of the experience of a building is to do with moving between different levels, and I reveal this possibility by making cuts in the section that can extend to the roof. The top floor and the roof are an opportunity to review the role of the building and its relationship to the city, which is why there are often gathering spaces at the top of our buildings. The section is also the device that mediates the light. Bringing light into the section is to do with the urban condition of the site and whether I want to create a sense of respite. When I am trying to introduce a certain quietness, I use zenithal light, from the roof. If the light conditions need to be more lively, I activate the section through the facade. Light has a decisive effect, creating an atmosphere of calm or encouraging enquiry – light in the section is the device to activate critical engagement.

_As I develop the section, I am trying to understand how to articulate the relationship between the skin of the building and the outside world, and how the facades register form. There is a dialogue as I consider whether the skin is closely related to the structural system or develops independently of it. Bypassing the structure gives me an opportunity to design a double facade, which can generate a moment of meaning between the external skin and the program. The gap between an external skin and an internal enclosure allows people to discover the section of the building at a single point, and can sometimes function as a circulation space. I first experimented with this arrangement in the design of houses, from Elektra to Pitch Black, and it figures in our public buildings, from the Idea Store Whitechapel to the NMAAHC. Moving through the gap is an opportunity to explore the relationship between the facade and the section, and it registers the entirety of the project. The gap is where you can understand the overall dimensions of a project and absorb this information without disturbing the continuity of the program. In our buildings, these vertical slots are where the dialogue happens between the purpose of the building and how that purpose is represented in the context of the city.

_When there is circulation in the gap, it takes on another story, another narrative. As a circulation system that operates independently of individual spaces, it has an orientation role and can augment the relationship between the interior and the context. By trapping the light, it becomes a register of the environment, a register of the place as an idea. Potentially, it mediates the environment and codifies a version of the public realm. In a complex example such as the NMAAHC, the space between the inner and outer walls of the Corona is fulfilling all these roles. The expression of the building is no longer about the additive program, as decoupling the core of the building from the outer facade allows the fundamental nature of the idea behind the functions to be expressed in the city. In public buildings one is searching for the meaning of the collective program, not the expression of the program itself. Elements of the program can come and go far more quickly than the facade is likely to change.

_Looking at the double facade arrangement in section, you can see the outline of one building standing inside a larger one, and the relationship between protected and protecting enclosures informs your experience at every level. Many shrines are organized this way – the double image relates to the idea that the house of the divinity can be represented in a construction that is part of the everyday world. Overlaying two enclosures is about architecture's ability to represent things at different scales, and shows how the full-size and the miniature versions can coexist. For me, this is one of the primary acts in architecture, and I am interested in removing it from ritualistic and shrine-like scenarios, which is where it originated. If the history of architecture over 10,000 years has been about this sacred doubling, what happens if it is made available to everyone? If we take that step, the doubling is no longer about separation and exclusion but about layers of information, layers of permeability, layers of intimacy. Due to its history, the concept of doubling is burnt into our psyche and our understanding; it is an organizational principle that is readily accessible to the perception of human beings and connects with the experience of our bodies in space.

Aïshti Foundation, Beirut, Lebanon, 2012–2015, facade detail   >

Location on Mediterranean waterfront   >>

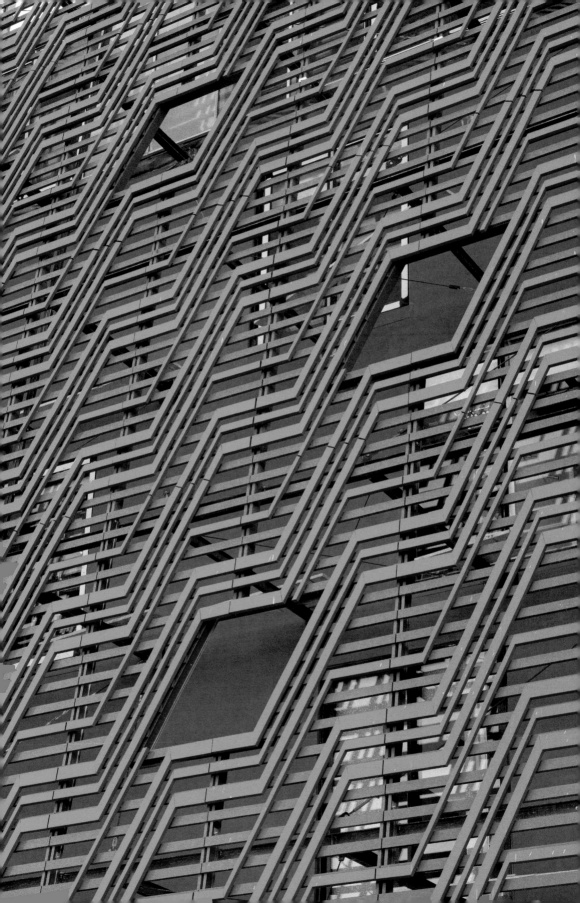

AÏSHTI FOUNDATION
BEIRUT, 2012–2015

Located to the north of the city center, the site was previously used for industrial purposes and stands between the coastal highway and the Mediterranean. The retail facilities function as an extension to the client's store on the adjacent site, and the museum houses his collection of contemporary art. Standing as close to the road as possible, the building forms a protective barrier between the road and a new landscaped space on the waterfront. The latticework facades protect the interior from the heat of the sun and unify the external appearance of the building.

Model and 1:1 mockup of facade   Location plan

< Position on the coastal highway, looking north

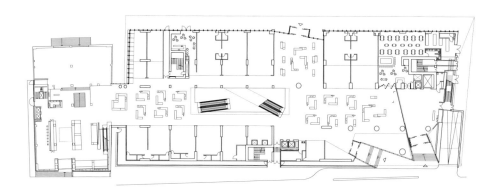

Ground-floor plan showing existing building (left) and entrance
to new building (right)

Atrium, looking up   Atrium, looking down

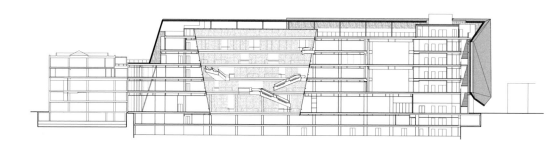

< Section showing existing building (left), atrium (center),
  and museum (right)

Gallery space

Internal window between gallery and retail space

Landscaped space on waterfront   >

Overview looking south to the city center   >>

ALARA CONCEPT STORE
LAGOS, 2011–2014

On a site in a coastal suburb, this design store was conceived as a destination in its own right, to distinguish it from other shops and markets in the city. In a tube-like enclosure, the stepped section can be used for display purposes and leads visitors to a roof deck, which has views of the surrounding buildings and landscape. The projecting ends of the concrete structure prevent direct sunlight reaching the interior, and latticework screens reduce glare when looking out of the building. Small, triangular windows pierce the walls and roof, and shine like jewels in the shaded space.

Model showing roof terrace

Location plan

‹ Front facade

Street view

›

Section

Stepped display space

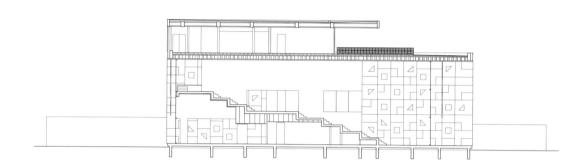

Roof terrace and view

Structural enclosure, triangular windows, and latticework facade

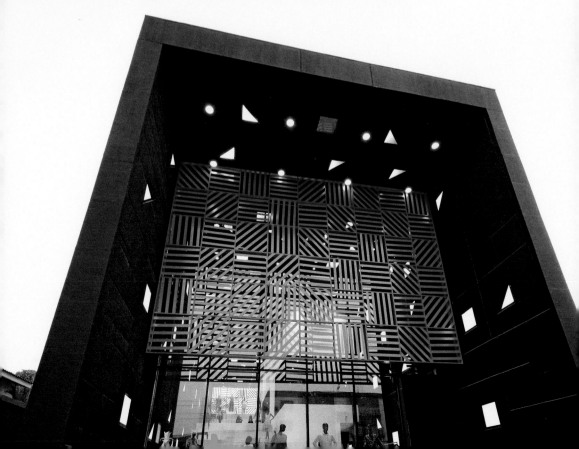

URBAN
SYSTEMS

_FLATTENING THE CODES

London has changed a great deal since we started work on the first public buildings in 2001. When they were commissioned, London was still a place where people were divided between those in the know and those on the outside, a city where you had access to information and ideas according to your education and status. My view was that the architecture of that period tended to play on this distinction. It was an architecture that set up hierarchies, talking about middle or upper class values, and I found that deeply problematic. I wanted to understand a condition that I was enjoying with my peers, which related to a more democratic London. This was a London that had flattened the codes and believed in open access, as I had experienced going to art school and the Royal College of Art. Our first public buildings were designed in response to that cultural and societal moment. The prevailing idea of architectural modernism in London was somewhat Iberian, with render finishes and recessed windows. After my travels in Spain and Portugal, I was not convinced about using this imagery in a more northerly climate. My approach was based on responding to the specific environments where the projects were located – to the luminosity of the place, to all the forces that were operating in the vicinity of the site. My aim was to democratize place through architecture, by displacing the codes that might privilege certain spaces. What I was proposing was that architecture had moved on from being a universal act of form making to being a specific response to a place and a time.

_For me, the wider urban context, and even the landscape, have always been basic considerations for understanding the place where you are located. As it happens, the city is very good at disguising the place you are in; by providing certain comforts and stabilities, it protects you from this basic information. This is all very well but great architecture covers both options: it acknowledges the place and gives you some protection from the reality of the location. What makes it great architecture is that it carefully lets you know the degree to which it is mediating the underlying situation. Why is that important? Understanding the role of mediation gives you a more exact picture of where you are in the world. This is the fundamental issue. I look at local buildings for what they say about the history and culture of the area. Some examples attract my attention more than others because they embody a particular form of construction to make a more general statement. The combination I am referring to can happen on any type of building, and when I see it, I am interested in the moment of transition, as one reading is superseded by another. I always take note of the public buildings in an area because they provide an inventory of the formal motifs that are already in circulation. The existing fabric is also a useful reference for understanding how material choices can affect the way in which light is expressed and articulated. Buildings in the vicinity of the site help me to understand the light – its intensity, luminosity or harshness – and the way in which some materials come to the fore and others are more recessive.

_In most places, street life speaks to the public realm, it shows how the public realm is being inhabited and the range of activities that are taking place there. Is it an area of artists' studios? Is it a place that is dedicated to movement and circulation, an area that is activated by markets, or somewhere that is completely different by day and by night? Is it a place where there are lots of clubs, empty in the daytime and alive at night? Is it an area where people are very casual about whether they are walking in the road or on a pavement? These are all psychological considerations that temper the way in which architecture presents itself. They are questions about how things happen in the public realm, how people connect with each other, and whether they work together or separately. When we are developing a project, there is always a melting moment between concerns that arise from a scrutiny of the public realm and concerns relating to the client's brief. This interface, at the moment when the issues on both sides are clear, has the most interesting potential for expression. The Idea Store Whitechapel illustrates one of these moments, as a public realm and a building fold into each other in a shared threshold – where the suspended atrium on the front facade overhangs the pavement below. This idea of the threshold as a space in which there is equivalence between two systems is one that I have explored in all our public buildings. The two systems have to be in balance, with one neither greater nor less than the other. Whether I am making a canopy, an overhang, a fold in the plane of the street, or stitching together various conditions, there has to be an equivalence between the two systems. I only feel that we have reached a resolution when I am confident that there will be a palpable tension between the systems.

— Our public buildings in London have a postcolonial content but they were also intended to present a new paradigm for the city. I think that you can see how a younger generation of architects has appropriated aspects of this work, not because of the postcolonial agenda but because of the democratizing shift that these buildings offered to communities. The postcolonial was the lens through which we looked to articulate and frame the discussion but, in the end, the projects were about the freedom of design to respond to the needs of communities and remove shackles. This is the political angle of architecture: to continually unshackle the present from the past. The creative stimulus was for these projects to make a garland of new institutions, suggesting an alternative, more democratic city. They were meant to be seen as a family of parts, operating with the existing fabric to create an alternative landscape.

— CONTINENTAL LIGHT

Working on the Museum of Contemporary Art Denver and the Moscow School of Management in Skolkovo, I had to develop my methodology to deal with situations that I had not encountered before. I found that I could read what was happening on and around both sites, but that my knowledge of the broader situation, which I had been able to take for granted in London, was incomplete. I needed to gather and organize this additional information, to frame my understanding of the maneuvers and shifts that I had observed at the architectural scale. Understanding that Denver is a place with blazing sun in the summer and tons of snow in the winter needed to be lodged in my mind before I could say, "Okay, there are these kids who ride bicycles and maybe they can just park their cycles under the building."

At that point my observations on the public realm at street level could be curated within a larger understanding.

_Sense of place was a critical consideration in Denver, because this museum was about cultivating an artistic community, which felt it had been diffused and had no central focus. As there was no open space at street level, the narrative of the whole building was to locate a public open space on the roof. The challenge in detail was how to weave public space through the miniature city that I created, which was the art museum. Our program was to weave through that city, discover an unexpected roofscape, arrive in a public plaza, and take in the context. The museum would be the only public building in this part of the city and we saw it as a gathering forum, with a strong three-dimensional relationship between the ground plane and roof level. The city is a mile high and we were amazed by the strength of the light and the atmosphere it gives. With so much natural light available, we organized the section to filter it through the walls, and channel it through the roof, to the heart of the plan. The amount of light required in the galleries, without using artificial light, was the generating issue. As light is the fundamental material of art and we were designing an arts institution, this was a convincing starting point.

_The Moscow situation was different again due to the peripheral location. Skolkovo, the location of the Moscow School of Management, is beyond the suburbs and, on my first encounter, the site was a forest, with its own ecology and springtime renewal. Here was a moment where architecture had not intervened and neutralized the sense of what the place could be – I was confronted very vividly with that realization. This encounter was such a powerful experience that, once we started work, I could not get it out of my head and it eventually forced us to develop a new design strategy. The idea of a large-scale building, in which all the activities of a campus occur, was the direct result of my emotional reaction to seeing the raw context of Moscow. On that first visit I saw the uncultivated Moscow – its wildness, its snow, its springs – and I felt that I could see where the city had come from. Having understood the site, I realized that we could use the winter snows, which can be ten feet deep, as a lens to the landscape. This thought led us to the cylinder, a building capable of looking in all directions, which was our starting point.

_The cylinder became the raised disc, containing public facilities and protecting the arrival points, and the architecture was no longer about a window to a view – as it had been in Whitechapel and Denver – but responded to a vast field. The type of articulations that we had made in earlier public buildings takes place in the four buildings – the program bars – above the disc. As there was so little development around the site, they respond to the direction of the light and create local context. The eastern tips of the bars have a beautiful coloration in the morning, as the west light does on the golden building, and the south-facing facades have an extraordinary luminosity, while the north facades are always cool. The School of Management is a very seasonal building. In winter it surveys the landscape and the effects of the weather, and in the summer it becomes a belvedere for the school community. From an internal function in the winter, directing the gaze toward the landscape, the disc is activated as a table in the spring and summer – that is the joy of it.

_PAVILION AND PLINTH

We opened the New York office in 2006 and our first project on Manhattan was Seven, which we developed as a generic urban section, before making it private. Compared with a site for a house in London, the urban context was incredibly dense and the development envelope, prescribed by the historic facade that we had to retain, put pressure on us to locate two stories below the level of the street. The discussion was about how to set up a permeable ground plane, allowing natural light to reach the lower floors, and how to combine this with a plinth, housing street-related activities – in our case, a gallery to display a selection of the client's art collection. The more private areas of the house are accommodated in two pavilions, standing on the plinth. The way in which you can use a site in an American city is largely determined by the law and your architectural approach has to take account of this. Seven prepared

Museum of Contemporary Art Denver, Denver, 2004–2007,
15th Street facade

Sugar Hill, New York, 2011–2014, looking downtown
from Highbridge Park

Moscow School of Management Skolkovo, Moscow, Russia,
2006–2010, natural and built form   >

National Museum of African American History and Culture,
Washington, DC, 2009–2016, the Capitol Hill axis looking east

us for doing the Sugar Hill building, whose section is broadly similar to that of the house.

_The first thing that struck me about Sugar Hill was the prominence of the site. It is in the northern section of Manhattan where you start to be aware of both the east and west sides of the island. Not far from the Harlem River, the site drops by twenty feet from one end to the other and our first move was to set up a plinth that would negotiate the difference. The plinth is a response to the geography and the need to adjust to the different ground levels, but its height refers to the three-story street architecture in this area. When the early farming settlements here first developed and the streets were laid out, this was the scale of the buildings and that datum is still visible in storefronts and older premises. Cities develop in layers and I was interested in how the mansion blocks in Upper Harlem differentiate the area from Lower Harlem, where the density of the brownstone buildings is lower. In Edgecombe, where our site is, the datum created by these mansion blocks is very strong, very noticeable.

_Above the street-level architecture, the height of the mansion blocks was the next cutoff, which is reflected by the terrace on the ninth floor of our building. The height of this terrace is the same as that of the mansion blocks built in the 1920s and 1930s, and the floors that rise above it address later developments in the city. Due to the roads and changes in level, it was difficult to avoid Sugar Hill becoming an object building. The prominence of the site forces the building to stand out, and as it is visible on four sides, we could not use the mansion blocks as a precedent, as they usually make street spaces. To counter this sense of isolation, our strategy was to make connections with the surrounding area that extended beyond the immediate physical context. As well as providing an entrance to the apartment tower, the podium houses a early childhood center and the Children's Museum of Art and Storytelling, organized around a series of small courtyards and light chambers in the same way as Seven.

_URBAN LANDSCAPES

In 2008 we were commissioned to design two neighborhood libraries in the southeast quadrant of Washington, DC, and in 2009 our team won the competition to design the National Museum of African American History and Culture (NMAAHC) on the National Mall. Both of these locations were very different from anywhere I had previously worked, but my experience of tropical cities, and how they engage with geography and the landscape, helped me to understand the city. The libraries had similar requirements but very different sites, and this was our starting point. In the suburb of Bellevue, the site of the William O. Lockridge Library is on land that is sloping away from the Potomac River, a condition reflected in the way that the organization of the building winds gently upward, taking in the view as it does so. The pavilions on the front facade look toward the center of the neighborhood, at the foot of the slope, but the whole building is moving up to a view in the other direction, over the gardens at the top of the slope. We had noticed that many of the residential buildings in the area have two parts, a solid base and a framed superstructure, and we tried to follow this pattern in the fabric of the library. This is the explanation for the vertical timber fins on the outside walls of the entrance pavilions. The local community did not give much significance to the way their houses were constructed but taking the ordinariness of an area and elevating it into a public building was a strategy we had followed in the Idea Store Whitechapel.

_The site for the Francis A. Gregory Library is completely flat and stands on the edge of one of the forest belts that cut through this section of the city. Alabama Avenue, the road in front of the library, connects several local communities. In this case, the trees and the horizontality of the landscape were the inspiration, and, reflecting the civic agenda common to both libraries, we conceived the building as a neoclassical pavilion, which would address the built context and the forest with equal weight. To hold its place on the road, the profile of the building is very assertive, but the materiality of the facade creates a large-scale moiré pattern that causes the building to merge with the forest. Historically, classicism was the preferred style for civic buildings in the eastern states, and the tone of the facades matches the shade beneath the trees.

_The National Mall, where we were working on the design of the NMAAHC, is one of the most stimulating environments that I have played in. I am always interested in the legibility of my buildings, and I was very concerned that the museum should not be reduced to something generic and ineffective – whatever we did needed to engage with history and the site, without being predictable. The National Mall has a powerful singularity, but as we studied it more carefully, the picture became more complex. The general layout and the architecture of several of the Smithsonian museums, and of the main monuments in the memorial park, are neoclassical in style but two of the earliest buildings, the Castle and the Washington Memorial, have Norman and Egyptian sources. The National Gallery of Art was the last completely classical museum to be completed, in 1941, and the museums built since then have taken a contemporary approach to dealing with their immediate context, while continuing to respect the geometry of the Mall. These later buildings include Gordon Bunshaft's Hirshhorn Museum whose floating drum reflects its central position on the south side of the Mall, and I. M. Pei's East Building whose triangulated forms are a response to the direction of nearby roads and the position of the Capitol. What I saw in the National Mall was a conversation between buildings with strong individual presences, adding layers of meaning to the original plan, which President Washington had commissioned from Major Pierre Charles L'Enfant in 1791.

_The impact of the buildings is dependent on the scale of the landscape, which extends from the banks of the Potomac River to the nearest hill, which is the site of the United States Capitol. Classified as a park, the dimensions of the National Mall are determined by the geography of the location: east to west, by the distance between the Lincoln Memorial, overlooking the river, and the Capitol; and north to south, by the distance between the Jefferson Memorial, overlooking the Tidal Basin, and the White House. The layout of the park involves bold devices – avenues of trees and distinctively shaped expanses of water – to give a sense of orientation, and local planting schemes that reflect the identity of individual buildings and monuments. If there is one construction that underpins the success of the park, it is the Washington Monument, designed by Robert Mills in 1836 and constructed between 1848 and 1884. The position and height operate with the geometry of the park to break the long dimensions, giving a greater sense of intimacy to the four main areas on each side of the monument.

_GEOGRAPHIC MARKERS

Our project takes a lead from both the architecture and land-scape of the National Mall. The position and height of the abo-veground volume are controlled by sight lines from buildings to the east and north. With identical facades, the Corona has the presence of a neoclassical pavilion, putting it in the same architectural family as the older museums and celebrating the position of our site on the corner between the Capital Hill and White House axes. On the facades, the pattern of the bronze finish screen is based on floral motifs found in historic iron-work in Charleston and New Orleans, a further reference to historic precedent, in this case involving black artisans. Archi-tectural details can be difficult to read on the Mall due to the distances involved, which is an issue that Bunshaft and Pei addressed by using powerful forms and reducing the level of visual detail. Compared with them, we have an intricate level of detailing on our facades, which registers as a continuous visu-al texture when seen from a distance.

_We are the closest museum to the Washington Monument, and, following its example, we employed a landscaped mound to situate our building in the larger context. The NMAAHC and the Washington Monument are in a transitional zone between the other museums to the east and the memorial park to the west, and the latticework facades acknowledge this transition, creating a dappled light in the same way as foliage. Tipping the planes of the facade forward strengthens this connection by breaking the profile of the museum at the corners, allowing light to fall on the back surface of the screen, and repeats the angle employed at the top of the Washington Monument. By acknowledging the geometry of the monument in our building, whose volume was determined by its more conventionally scaled neighbors, I wanted to draw attention to the cultural origins of the memorial and the continuity between the African and European sources.

_Washington has a subtropical climate with cool winters and hot, humid summers. Angling the planes of the facade forward reduces their exposure to direct sunlight in the summer, which protects the interior of the building from overheating. As the volume we could build above ground was limited, 50 percent of the museum had to be constructed at a lower level, and the gap between the outer and inner facades of the Corona draws natural light into the subterranean chamber. The general organization of the section is similar to the Seven and Sugar Hill buildings, but in this case the podium is below grade. Like the internal courts in those projects, the Contemplative Court admits light to the sunken podium, and the Oculus, which is set in the ground to the north of the Corona, marks the position of the court and the extent of the lower level galleries.

_Of the buildings and monuments that contribute to the National Mall, the Washington Monument is the only one with sufficient stature to register at the geographic scale, and its tapered surfaces are a sympathetic foil to the natural and man-made forms that constitute the National Mall. By organizing the facades of our building as a stack of angled planes, I wanted to generalize the architecture of the museum to a degree where, despite the restriction on its size, it would take on a similar function in deflecting attention to the surroundings and the wider context. This was one of several strategies we pursued on the National Mall, while in Beirut, working on the Aïshti Foundation, our main focus was to design a building that would register at the scale of the sweeping bay to the north of the central area.

_The program for the Aïshti Foundation involved bringing together a retail facility and a museum of contemporary art, and the creation of a new landscaped space for the city. Beirut has the Mediterranean on two sides, but as you move away from the center, there is little public infrastructure on the waterfront. Many of the sites are used for industry and cut off by the coastal highway, and these systems close you off from experiencing the microclimate on the water's edge – that beautiful temperature you have on the coast. Our building takes one of these industrial sites and, by protecting the waterfront from the road, makes a public place in a new location. The latticework cladding neutralizes the detailed expression of the program, and the resulting form is visible at the geographic scale. When you approach the site, the building functions as a gateway to the waterfront, but, unlike a normal gateway, we made a funnel that is narrower on the road side and opens up toward the landscape and the view. That was the challenge: to give the building presence at the scale of the bay and make a gateway to this park and the incredible view.

_In Denver we wanted to register the altitude and make a public place in a city that has few of them; the Moscow School of Management Skolkovo was about working with the climate and with a culture that has a collective identity; and Sugar Hill develops a relationship between the public realm and a private citadel – the residential tower. In designing the NMAAHC, we made relationships at every scale, from the landscape dominated by the Washington Monument to the neoclassical buildings next to the site, and in Beirut we created a park in a dramatic location that had previously been inaccessible.

PIETY BRIDGE AND WHARF, NEW ORLEANS, 2008–2014

Piety Street runs toward the Mississippi, but until recently the residents of this area were unable to access the river due to a flood wall, running alongside a railway line, and the wharves that previously occupied the waterfront. With the demise of the wharves, Crescent Park was created alongside the river. Complementing the park, the timber substructure for the old Piety Wharf now supports a recreational deck overlooking the river, and Piety Bridge connects the residential area to the park and the deck. Both the bridge, and the walls and barriers that enclose the deck, are constructed of Corten steel.

Model

Location plan

< Corten steel structure and timber stair

View of Mississippi River with Piety Bridge (left) and the gable wall of the old Piety Wharf (right)

>

View from Piety Street

Assembling prefabricated sections of bridge

View from Piety Bridge towards Crescent City
Connection bridges   ›

Crescent Park with Piety Bridge and Piety Wharf (left)

Piety Wharf seen from the top of Piety Bridge   ››

Approach from Crescent Park

Entrance showing Corten steel walls and screen

Site plan showing grid of existing timber structure

Old gable wall with opening to view

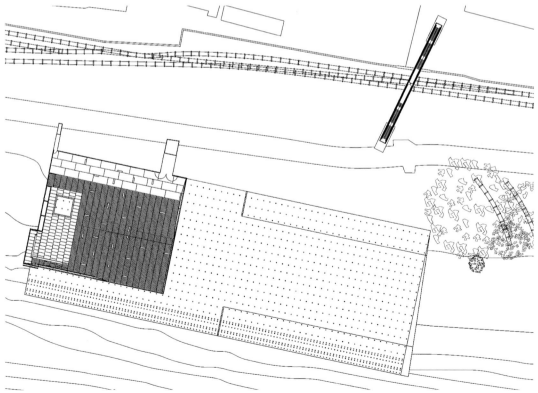

PIETY BRIDGE AND WHARF

Gable wall from deck

Platform with framed opening to existing
structure and river   >

Night view looking toward the central business district   >>

BIENNALE CITY

In 2014 I was approached by Okwui Enwezor to collaborate on the 2015 Biennale. He was the director that year and his vision involved bringing a series of modern projects from the art world into a single assembly, to be shown at the Biennale's two main venues. The Central Pavilion in the Giardini Gardens was built in 1894 and is the location for the major thematic exhibition presented by each director. A short walk away is the Arsenale, part of Venice's historic shipyard, where Enwezor was planning a second exhibition complementing the first. The main space here is in the 316-meter-long building, dating from 1303 and rebuilt in the sixteenth century, which was used for manufacturing ropes. The Central Pavilion was conceived as a neoclassical building but has been extended and modified at various points in its history.

THE ARSENALE

I immediately engaged with the prospect of working in the Arsenale because most of the exhibitions that I had seen there were overwhelmed by the artifact-like character of this brick building with its 21-meter-long timber roof trusses. My hunch was that our intervention would have to work alongside the existing architecture, to transform the perception of the halls and provide physical support for the art works. I had been looking at previous biennale designs and was struck by the Italian architect Paulo Portoghesi's intervention at the Arsenale in 1980, when he created a representation of the postmodernist city, complete with its own iconography. Under the title *Strada Novissima,* he organized a street running through the entire building, with continuous facades on both side and doorways leading into individual spaces. I was taken with his understanding that two- and three-story buildings could sit comfortably in the section of the old building but decided to make a different test. I had previously designed the Museum of Contemporary Art Denver, based on enclosing an abstract version of the pedestrian city, and a series of installations in collaboration with individual artists. With these projects in mind, I was drawn to the notion of a scaled-down city, extending over the full length of the space. The continuity of the historic halls would give the sense of a sequential narrative and, by reducing the scale, I would be able to represent a variety of urban conditions. Rather than a single street, I was interested in recreating the experience of Venice as a series of compressions, expansions, densities, movements, and labyrinths, together with memories of gardens, squares, a chapel, and a citadel.

_In practice, these features were realized as a pattern of spaces whose abstraction neutralized the architecture of the halls and made a backdrop for the art itself. Our intervention does not touch the external walls; they are entirely visible in their raw state, and, with the massive brick columns and the existing doorways, they are the residue of the real Venice. The details of the existing fabric are experienced in relatively intimate spaces, as fragments whose impact on viewing conditions is more controlled than when they are fully visible. This was the strategy that I first presented to Enwezor – the drawings were quite diagrammatic, but that was the starting point.

_Looking at the dimensions of the empty halls, there was some variation in their lengths and, at the same time, a repetitive rhythm to the experience of moving through them. Our proposal offers a counterpoint to the geometry of the halls while taking into account the display requirements of the artists that Enwezor had in mind. Using a system of self-supporting walls, the occupation patterns in each of the main spaces evoke the spatial experiences associated with different areas of the city. By way of introduction, you enter into the one space that is completely open, a civic square with four symmetrically disposed columns. This is the only chamber in which the structure of the original building is fully revealed, but the brickwork of the columns has been given a neutralizing wrap, to avoid any distraction from the art works. From here you progress to what I call the administration quarter, arranged on either side of a grand boulevard. As I see it, the soft but really important narrative to the work that Enwezor had envisaged was that all the artists related to an urban condition and the notion of cities. The works in the boulevard, for example, were like members of a choir, singing in different combinations up and down the space, and the boulevard was the activator of that possibility. To either side you have the different administrations, which are more enclosed and give each artist a separate space. The boulevard terminates in the opposite condition to the civic square: an equivalent space representing a garden, given over to a sweeping polychromatic work by Katharina Grosse.

_Like nature, Grosse's work envelops the entire space, wrapping itself round the columns and creating a transition to the labyrinth in the next hall, which I saw as a residential quarter in Venice. The way in which small squares open up to give longer views, houses appear one behind the other, and you go under one building to reach the next: these are the experiences we had in mind. In our scheme there is a network of routes that finds its way through the center and other routes that relate to the perimeter walls and their historic brickwork. In keeping with the residential theme, you eventually discover a little square and the facade of a chapel. Passing through the facade, there is the most extraordinary treasure inside. This is the octagonal space for the installation of Chris Ofili's work – in terms of the city, it represents the way in which the ecclesiastic infrastructure is integrated with everyday life.

_Entering the next hall, you were approaching the midpoint of the exhibition and, after the intensity of the previous sections, my intuition was to slow the pace and give people an opportunity to gather their thoughts. I was thinking of the informal sequences of linked squares and courtyards that you find in Venice, where there is no privileged view and people can negotiate the spaces in anyway they choose. The relative openness of our spaces suited the reflective qualities of the work displayed here, and the informality of this section complemented the unexpected formality of the next hall, which I characterized as a formal landscape.

_I had said to Enwezor that I wanted to make one space where there would be no orthogonals and no interconnected walls. In other words, we would only use freestanding planes and they could not be positioned at right angles to, or parallel with, the walls of the building. It was a kind of experiment that gave us a space of perspectives, in which the compressions and

< **Arsenale**

Hall with brick columns

Installation work in progress

Little square

Formal landscape

Central Pavilion

Forming the Arena space

The Arena

expansions resulting from a limited number of moves created unexpected opportunities. At first sight the spaces we created appeared to have a leftover character, but they were also highly occupiable. For me, it was about the power of fragment spaces, which is something I have always been interested in. This connected with the way in which artists are able to appropriate found spaces and turn them to their own uses – I was looking for a condition where you would feel that the artworks had just happened upon a condition that was uniquely suited to them. Where everything had been orthogonal to this point, I wanted to introduce a new geometry that would raise people's expectations as they moved into the second half of the exhibition.

_In the final hall on the main axis, you entered a second labyrinth, symmetrically placed with the earlier one but less extensive. Our sequence ends in a space that is enclosed by tall walls, representing the citadel. This is the location of the cathedral, which is where we showed Georg Baselitz's work. His monumental paintings speak about the body, and about life and death. They also make me think of the important public spaces in cities that have no function other than to talk about phenomenal issues. The space for the paintings was a second octagon, with a larger scale than the first and cracked through the middle – broken into displaced halves to allow access from either side. The cathedral standing in an urban space was the conclusion to our work in the main halls. There are three further spaces on a secondary axis that we cleaned up and added some lights to. They did not have the brick columns that march along the Arsenale's main axis and the artists' work could be displayed openly without the risk of being overwhelmed by the architecture.

_I was working on the design for the Arsenale at the same time as Enwezor was bringing together the artists who would occupy the spaces. When I was ready, he was close to finalizing the list, and we began a process of adjustment to bring things together. What was surprising was to see how few changes were needed. I talked him through the spaces and he would say this work would look good in that location or that someone else might like a certain condition. The changes we made were not to the overall pattern but to the size of individual spaces, to accommodate the work in question. The two labyrinths were well suited to projection and acoustic work or for separating off work that needed to be seen on its own. I thought that the hall with the angled, freestanding walls would be the most problematic, but it was Enwezor's favorite space; when he saw it he was immediately excited about the flexibility it gave him.

_THE CENTRAL PAVILION

Enwezor's brief for the Central Pavilion was quite different from the premise at the Arsenale. He was interested in presenting a six-month-long cycle of performances as part of the thematic exhibition, and our first task was to investigate how this might be accommodated within the existing hierarchy of spaces. Besides finding a space that was the right size, it would somehow need to complement the displays in the surrounding galleries. The Arena, as it was later named, was to be the place where performance and visual art would overlap, providing a respite space where people could reflect on their experiences at the Biennale. Enwezor was looking for a place of discourse and exchange at the heart of the project, whose existence would have implications for all the exhibitions in his program.

_I went back to the original plans of the building and noticed that the gallery on the entrance axis had originally been significantly longer than it is now. The current mezzanine level, which effectively shortens this space, was a later intervention. When we looked more closely, we found that the roof structure continued over the whole area, and, to return to the earlier footprint, we decided to remove the wall that separated the mezzanine from the gallery. This gave us the highest single space in the Central Pavilion, a double-height space with a comparable scale to that of the Arsenale. In relation to the emerging brief for the Arena, it gave me a sufficiently generous industrial scale to make an architectural intervention that would sit comfortably beneath the existing roof.

_I took down the wall and cleaned up the remaining fabric, creating the possibility of a performance space that could be accessed directly from the entrance to the building, or from either side. We eventually decided that access from the main entrance was too direct and made a new route into the building by cutting through several service spaces. Smaller in scale and with no natural lighting, these spaces were used to show projection works, which alluded to the performance theme in the Arena. In this scenario, the entrances to the Arena were on a transverse axis linking the Carlo Scarpa garden and a gallery at the center of building that we saw as a kind of courtyard. To emphasize the significance of this space, we introduced free-standing cross-walls to reduce the scale of the adjacent galleries. The courtyard space was intended to shift the center of gravity of the entire plan in the direction of successive extensions to the building, after it was first completed.

_The brief for the Arena was that it would be the setting for the performance cycles and for one-off events relating to the themes of the Biennale. The most notable of the daily performances were the continuous readings of the English translation of Karl Marx's *Das Kapital,* which was curated by Isaac Julien. In the early stages, we considered different seating capacities and various sight lines, which convinced me that we did not need to remove the mezzanine floor, along with the wall I mentioned earlier. Leaving the mezzanine in place allowed us to have a more intimate chamber suited to the daily performances, overlooked by tiered seating at the upper level. The tiered seating gave a privileged view of events in the chamber and could accommodate a larger audience when required. With this combination we had a performance space that worked in the round and, with the upper level, the possibility of the single orientation you have in a theater.

_In my mind, the form of the lower, more intimate space goes back to the ecclesia, the gathering space in ancient Athens. It was intended to encourage debate and connects with a line of enquiry in our buildings concerning the role of gathering chambers in institutions and in constructed public places. The critical question is how you break the narrative of the constructed public experience, to make it singular. When people come together, it is the singular experience of the collective condition that is significant. This is very relevant in a situation where you have a highly curated art experience, and I am attracted to an intimacy based on the emotional connectedness that comes from a tiering system, which allows for visual and oral relationships. Our intention was to activate an awareness of the role of such spaces and their relevance to the premise of Enwezor's vision for the Biennale. We hoped that the opportunity for people to focus on the meta-structure of the curatorial vision would give them a sense of their own position and recondition their view of the work itself. I see this as the basis for a new connectivity, and as a way of encouraging public engagement.

_We also carried out work in the octagonal entrance chamber, so that Enwezor could install several works by Fabio Mauri there. Besides blocking off the doorway on the main axis and making a smaller entrance in the sidewall, we planted shallow projecting panels on the four angled walls of this space. Like our self-supporting walls at the Arsenale, the panels muted the architectural details in the octagon, to allow the contemporary implications of Mauri's work to register in this historic space. Enwezor felt that Mauri's readings would, for an Italian audience, connect with the origins of the Central Pavilion and its history. The chapel and cathedral spaces we organized at the Arsenale reflected the geometry of this space.

_Working in the Arsenale, we needed to pursue a strategy that would establish a balance between the architectural power of the ancient halls and the work of the artists. In the Central Pavilion, our approach was more archeological. We researched the history of the building and took this into consideration in each of our interventions. The city played a part at both venues. Our scheme for the Arsenale developed from a concern with the settlement pattern of the city and its materiality. Introducing the Arena to the Central Pavilion involved the partial renewal of an urban institution that continues to play a critical role in the contemporary world.

BIENNALE CITY

VENICE 2015

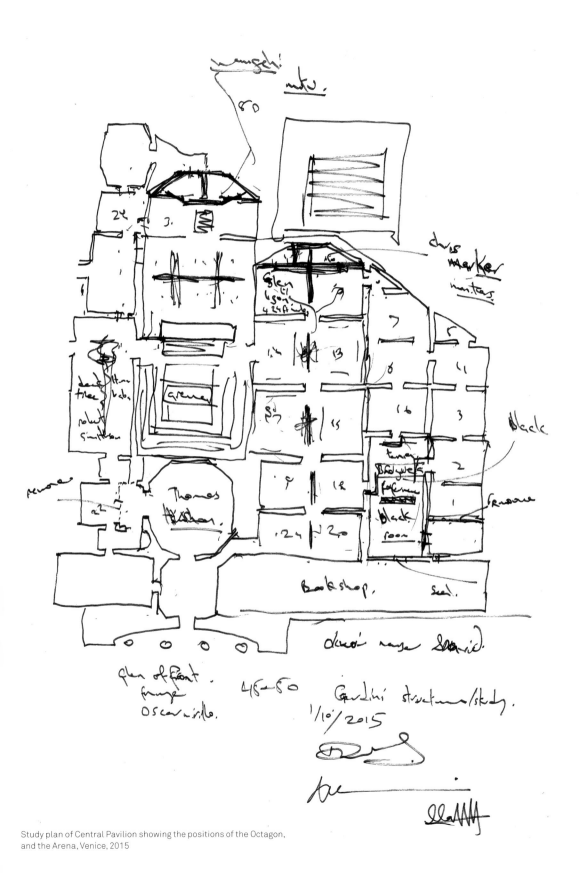

Study plan of Central Pavilion showing the positions of the Octagon,
and the Arena, Venice, 2015

Neutralizing the brick columns in the civic square

The civic square lit by neon works

The grand boulevard

In the administrative quarter

Garden

First labyrinth

The chapel

Entering the linked squares and courtyards

The formal landscape

Second labyrinth

The walls of the citadel

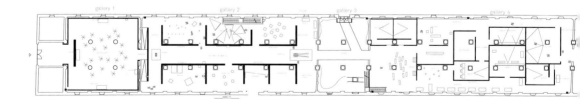

In the cathedral

Plan showing positions of the civic square (left), the chapel (center), and the cathedral (right)

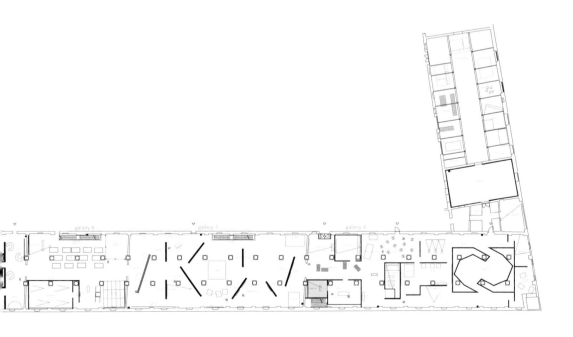

Entrance facade

The Octagon

The first gallery with doorways to the Carlo Scarpa
garden (left) and the Arena (right)

Forming the Arena space

Upper- and lower-level seating, Arena

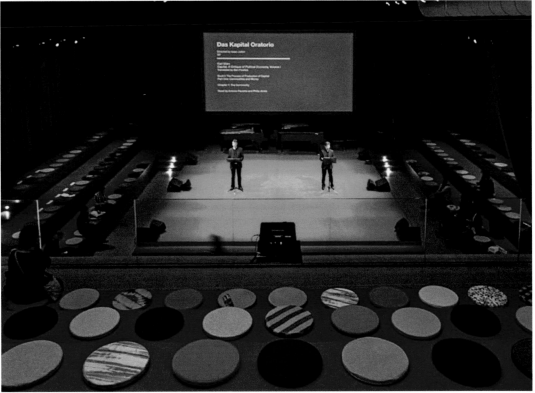

The ecclesia

Performance of *Das Kapital Oratorio* curated by Isaac Julien

The intimate chamber and the privileged view >

Performance of *Work Songs*, compiled by Jason Moran and >>
Alicia Hall Moran

Performance of *Work Songs* viewed from the upper level

The courtyard gallery with doorways to split galleries (next page)

Gallery with new screen wall on cross axis

New screen wall dividing doorway

The Dissolve, installation for SITE Santa Fe Eight International Biennial, Santa Fe, New Mexico, 2010

Olowe of Ise (Yoruba, ca. 1875–ca. 1938), veranda post
with caryatid, Museum Fünf Kontinente, Munich

DAVID ADJAYE

David Adjaye OBE is recognized as a leading architect of his generation. He was born in Tanzania to Ghanaian parents, and his influences range from contemporary art, music, and science to African art forms and the civic life of cities. In 1994 he set up his first office, where his ingenious use of materials and his sculptural ability established him as an architect with an artist's sensibility and vision.

He frequently collaborates with contemporary artists on art and installation projects. Examples include *The Upper Room,* with thirteen paintings by Chris Ofili, 2002, *Within Reach,* a second installation with Ofili in the British pavilion at the Venice Biennale, 2003, and the Thyssen-Bornemisza Art for the 21st Century Pavilion, which was designed to show a projection work by Olafur Eliasson, *Your black horizon,* at the 2005 Venice Biennale. *The Upper Room* is now in the permanent collection of Tate Britain. In 2015, he collaborated with Okwui Enwezor on the design of the 56th Venice Art Biennale.

Adjaye has taught at the Royal College of Art, where he previously studied, and at the Architectural Association School in London, and has held distinguished professorships at the universities of Pennsylvania, Yale, and Princeton. At Harvard, he was the John C. Portman Design Critic in Architecture and received the W. E. B. Du Bois Medal for outstanding work in the field of African and African American studies in 2014. He was awarded the OBE for services to architecture in 2007, and received the Design Miami / Year of the Artist title in 2011, the Wall Street Journal Innovator Award in 2013, and the London Design Medal in 2016. Adjaye Associates has offices in London and New York.

IMAGE CREDITS

Unless otherwise stated, all drawings, model views, and photographs of projects designed by David Adjaye appear courtesy of Adjaye Associates. The following credits apply to all images for which separate acknowledgement is due.

5, 41 center left, 51 top, 53 bottom, 54, 66 bottom, 67 bottom, 76–77, 80–82 top, 104, 106, 113, 115 top, 118 top, 123–125 top, 130 bottom right, 131 top, 143, 149, 159 top left, 231 top left, 263 top, 288 top right and bottom, 289 bottom, 296 bottom–305, 306 bottom–313 Ed Reeve

10–11 Sum (SumProject+SumResearch)

16–17, 21–33, 47, 52 bottom, 53 top, 73, 103, 218–223, 295 David Adjaye

40 bottom, p. 50 bottom, 51 bottom, p. 66 top, 195, 241, 251, 271 Wilfried Petzi/HDK

40 top Daniela Pellegrini

41 bottom, 97 bottom, 189 top right, 238–240, 242–249 Julien Lanoo

41 top Knoll

48–49, 67 top left and right, 75, 78–79, 82 bottom, 84, 86–88, 105, 114, 115 bottom–117, 118 bottom–119, 121 top left and bottom, 130 bottom left, 158, 159 top center, 189 bottom, 230 top, 231 bottom, 314–315 Lyndon Douglas

57 bottom Peter Sharpe

57 top Alex MacLennan

58 bottom Jakob Polacsek

58 top Group 22

59 Kyungsub Shin

83 James Wang

85 Xia Zhi

89 Stephen Jameson

97 top right, 137–142, 144–147, 150–151, 198 bottom, 201 top, 203–205, 207, 211, 262 bottom Wade Zimmerman

110–112 top, 112 top Tim Soar

120, 121 top right, 164–167, 176–177, 179, 188, 230 bottom, 231 top right Edmund Sumner

122, 130 top, 262 top Dean Kauffman

125 bottom Iwan Baan

131 bottom, 159 bottom, 189 top left, 194, 196–197, 199 bottom, 206, 208–209, 214–215, 263 bottom Alan Karchmer/NMAAHC

168–175, 178 top Jeffrey Sauers

180–181 Maxine Schnitzer

210 Marc McQuade

213 bottom Dorian Shy

216–217 Darren Bradley

250, 252–255 Studio Hans Wilschut

270, 272–273, 275 bottom, 279 top, 280 bottom, 282–283 Tim Hursley

237 Guillaume Ziccarelli/Aïshti Foundation

274 top, 275 top, 276–278 top, 279 bottom, 280 top, 281 Eskew+Dumez+Ripple

316 Heini Schneebeli